HOW TO HEAL FROM HEARTBREAK

A BREAKUP RECOVERY GUIDE ANYONE CAN
USE TO BUILD RESILIENCE, DEVELOP HEALTHY
COPING HABITS, & FEEL CONFIDENT AGAIN

T.J. ODINSON

CONTENTS

INTRODUCTION

When someone leaves, it's because someone else is about to arrive.

— PAULO COELHO

Have you ever experienced that gut-wrenching sensation when someone you deeply cared about walked away, leaving you feeling like you're standing on unstable ground? It's like the world suddenly flips upside down, and you're left grappling with emotions you never knew existed. If you've nodded along or felt a pang in your chest just reading this, then you're not alone. Heartbreak is a universal human experience, and let's face it, it's downright brutal. But here's the thing—it's also profoundly transformative.

Picture this: You're sitting alone, surrounded by the debris of what once was, wondering how you'll ever find the strength to piece yourself back together. Whether it's a romantic breakup, the end of a friendship, or even the loss of a cherished dream, the pain cuts deep. But amidst this chaos, there lies an opportunity—an opportunity to heal, to grow, and to emerge stronger than you ever thought possible.

Like superheroes emerging from adversity, you have the power to turn your pain into strength. Every setback becomes a stepping stone, every tear a testament to your resilience.

I get it. Really, I do. The weight of grief can feel like an anchor dragging you deeper into the abyss of despair. It's as if the world has dimmed its lights, and you're stumbling in the darkness, searching for a glimmer of hope. And that sense of loss? It's not just a feeling; it's a relentless wave crashing against the shores of your soul, threatening to engulf you in its depths.

Letting go? Easier said than done, right? Whether it's someone who's physically gone or someone who should no longer occupy space in your heart, the process feels like tearing away a piece of yourself. It's agonizing, messy, and downright confusing. How do you sever ties when every fiber of your being screams for their presence?

And then there's the identity crisis. Who are you without them? Without that relationship, that title, that role you played so well? It's like staring into a mirror and seeing a stranger staring back at you. But let me remind you—your worth isn't tethered to someone else's presence or absence. You are whole, worthy, and deserving of love, regardless of who walks beside you.

Feeling stuck is like being trapped in quicksand—the more you struggle, the deeper you sink. You're desperate for solid ground, for a lifeline to pull you out of this suffocating rut. But what if I told you that this moment, this pain, is the catalyst for your transformation? It's not about just surviving; it's about thriving. It's about using this darkness as fuel to ignite the flames of growth within you.

And as for feeling lost? Trust me, I've been there. It's like wandering through a dense forest with no map, no compass, and no sense of direction. But here's the thing—sometimes, getting lost is the only way to find yourself.

In this book, you won't just find solace—you'll discover shortcuts to reclaiming your life and emerging more vital than ever. Meet the RECLAIM method, your roadmap to healing:

R: Recognize the Hurt—Acknowledge your pain and its source.

E: Embrace Forgiveness—Release yourself from the chains of resentment.

C: Channel Your Heartbreak Energy—Transform pain into power.

L: Liberate Your Inner Self—Break free from self-imposed limitations.

A: Assemble Your Heart—Piece together a stronger, wiser version of yourself.

I: Ignite Your Power—Tap into your inner strength and resilience.

M: Monumentalize Your Healing—Celebrate your journey and newfound resilience.

With these principles as your guide, you'll navigate through the darkness of heartbreak with newfound clarity and purpose.

Well, let me tell you a bit about myself. I'm T.J. Odinson, and I'm here to be your guide through the twists and turns of life's journey.

I've walked through my fair share of challenges and

triumphs, just like you. And through it all, I've made it my mission to not only overcome obstacles but to empower others to do the same. My journey has taught me invaluable lessons about resilience, self-discovery, and the power of the human spirit.

You see, I'm not just a writer—I'm someone who's been in the trenches, battling through the ups and downs of life. And that's what makes my approach to self-help different. It's not just theory; it's practical wisdom drawn from real-life experiences.

My motivation for writing this book? It's simple—I want to share what I've learned along the way in the hopes that it will light the way for others. I want to be the voice of encouragement when you're feeling lost, the cheerleader on your journey to personal growth.

If you're craving real-life insights, practical strategies, and a compassionate guide to navigate life's toughest moments, then look no further. This isn't just any book—it's your roadmap to resilience, written by someone who's been there, done that, and is here to light your path forward.

R—RECOGNIZE THE HURT

Some people believe holding on and hanging in there are signs of great strength. However, there are times when it takes much more strength to know when to let go and then do it.

— ANN LANDERS

You see, healing doesn't begin with sweeping emotions under the rug or pretending everything's okay. No, it starts with the courage to face your feelings head-on, to acknowledge the pain coursing through your veins, and to embrace the truth staring back at you in the mirror.

This chapter isn't about sugar-coating reality or offering quick fixes. It's about something far more profound—the raw, unfiltered journey of self-discovery that begins with recognizing the hurt. It's about giving yourself permission to feel, to grieve, and to honor the weight of what you've endured.

So, if you're ready to peel back the layers, to unearth the buried emotions, and to take that courageous first step toward healing, then buckle up—because we're about to embark on a journey of introspection, empathy, and ultimately, transformation. Together, we'll navigate the murky waters of heartbreak, armed with nothing but our vulnerability and the unwavering belief that healing is not just possible, but inevitable.

What Does It Mean to Let Go?

Letting go—it's a phrase we've all heard a million times, but what does it really mean? Is it as simple as unclenching your fists and releasing whatever's been weighing you down? Well, yes and no. Let's unpack this together.

First off, let's address the elephant in the room—what exactly are we letting go of? In the context of heartbreak, it's often a mix of emotions, memories, and attachments that have become intertwined with our sense of self. It could be the lingering hope of reconciliation, the bitterness of betrayal, or even just the comfort of familiarity. Letting go means untangling ourselves from these emotional knots, one by one, until we're free to move forward unencumbered.

Now, here's where things get tricky—misconceptions about letting go. One common myth is that letting go means forgetting, erasing, or denying the past. But that couldn't be further from the truth. Letting go isn't about pretending the pain never existed; it's about acknowledging it, honoring it, and then consciously choosing to release its hold over us. It's about making peace with the past without letting it define our future.

Another misconception is that letting go is a sign of weakness. Some people equate holding on with strength, as if clinging desperately to the past somehow makes us tougher. But here's the reality—it takes far more strength to loosen our grip, to surrender control, and to trust in the process of healing. Letting go isn't a surrender; it's a declaration of resilience, a testament to our capacity for growth and renewal.

Some people also think that letting go means we have to stop feeling our emotions altogether. Some people mistakenly think that letting go requires us to suppress or numb our feelings, as if pretending everything is fine will somehow make the pain disappear. But emotions are messy, complex, and inherently human. Trying to shut them off completely is like trying to stop the tide from coming in—futile and ultimately self-destructive.

Letting go isn't about becoming emotionless; it's about learning to navigate our emotions in a healthy and constructive way. It's about allowing ourselves to feel the full spectrum of human experience—the joy, the sorrow, the anger, and the love—without letting any single emotion define us.

So, why is letting go crucial to the healing process? Well, imagine trying to run a marathon with a ball and chain strapped to your ankle. It's not impossible, but it sure makes things a whole lot harder. Similarly, holding on to past hurts, resentments, and regrets weighs us down, draining our energy and hindering our progress. Letting go, on the other hand, sets us free—free to breathe, free to heal, and free to embrace the possibilities that lie ahead.

But let me be clear—letting go isn't a one-and-done deal. It's a continuous process, a series of small acts of courage and surrender, repeated day in and day out. It's okay if you stumble along the way, if you find yourself clinging to old wounds or slipping back into familiar patterns. Healing isn't linear, and neither is letting go. What matters is that you keep showing up, keep leaning into the discomfort, and keep choosing growth over stagnation.

So, my friend, take a deep breath and repeat after me— letting go isn't giving up; it's making space for something better. It's the first step toward reclaiming your power, your joy, and your sense of self. And trust me, the view from the other side of letting go? It's worth every ounce of courage it takes to get there.

Why It's Difficult to Let Go?

Alright, let's get real for a moment—letting go? Yeah, it's not exactly a walk in the park. In fact, it's more like trying to wrangle a herd of cats while juggling flaming torches. But hey, guess what? You're not alone in feeling this way. Letting go is hard—like, really hard—and there's a whole bunch of reasons why.

First off, let's talk about attachments. Whether it's a person, a place, or a dream we've been clinging to, letting go means severing ties with something that's become deeply intertwined with our sense of self. It's like trying to rip off a Band-Aid that's been stuck on for way too long—painful, messy, and downright terrifying.

Then there's the fear factor. Letting go means stepping into the unknown, venturing into uncharted territory without a map or a compass. It's natural to feel apprehensive about what lies on the other side of goodbye—will we be okay? Will we ever find something or someone to fill the void left behind? These questions can send our anxiety levels through the roof, making it even harder to take that leap of faith.

And let's not forget about pride. Admitting that we need to let go of something—whether it's a toxic relationship, an unattainable goal, or an outdated belief system—can feel like a blow to our ego. We may worry about what others will think, or we may cling stubbornly to the idea that we can tough it out on our own. But here's the thing—asking for help, admitting vulnerability, and acknowledging our limitations? That's not weakness; that's strength in its purest form.

But perhaps the biggest challenge of all is the emotional baggage we carry with us. Letting go requires us to confront our pain, our regrets, and our deepest fears head-on. It means facing the demons we've been avoiding, dredging up old wounds, and allowing ourselves to feel the full force of our grief. And let me tell you, that's no easy feat.

But here's the silver lining—nobody finds letting go easy. Seriously, not a single person on this planet breezes through the process without a hitch. We're all stumbling along, tripping over our own insecurities and doubts, wondering if we'll ever find solid ground again. So, if you're feeling overwhelmed, confused, or just plain exhausted by the idea of letting go, take heart—you're in good company.

The truth is, letting go is a messy, imperfect, and downright uncomfortable process. But you know what else it is? It's necessary. It's essential for our growth, our happiness, and our overall well-being. So, even when it feels like you're wading through quicksand, even when it seems like the weight of the world is bearing down on your shoulders, keep going. Keep taking those small steps forward, even if they feel like stumbling blocks. Because one day, you'll look back and realize that every struggle, every tear, and every moment of doubt was leading you toward something greater

—toward a life filled with freedom, joy, and limitless possibility.

How to Know When to Let Go

Alright, let's talk turkey—or in this case, relationships. Because not all relationships are meant to last forever. Sometimes, despite our best efforts and deepest desires, it's for the best that things come to an end. But how do you know when it's time to let go? Let's dive in.

First and foremost, trust your gut. Your intuition is a powerful tool, and it's usually pretty good at telling you when something isn't quite right. If your relationship leaves you feeling drained, anxious, or constantly on edge, that's a red flag. Healthy relationships should uplift you, not weigh you down.

Pay attention to how you feel when you're around the other person. Are you constantly walking on eggshells, afraid to speak your mind or be yourself? Do you find yourself making excuses for their behavior or rationalizing away your own feelings? If so, it might be time to take a step back and reassess whether this relationship is truly serving your best interests.

Next up, take a long, hard look at the dynamics of your relationship. Are you both on the same page when it comes to important issues like communication, trust, and respect? Do you feel heard, valued, and appreciated? Healthy relationships are built on a foundation of mutual respect and understanding, so if these elements are missing, it might be a sign that it's time to let go.

And let's not forget about boundaries. Healthy relationships require clear boundaries—boundaries that are respected and upheld by both parties. If your boundaries are constantly being violated or disregarded, that's a major warning sign that this relationship may not be worth holding on to.

Now, I know what you're thinking—letting go is easier said than done, especially when you've invested time, energy, and emotions into a relationship. But here's the thing—holding on to a toxic or unhealthy relationship isn't just detrimental to your well-being; it's also a disservice to both parties involved.

Remember, it's okay to prioritize your own happiness and emotional health. You deserve to be in a relationship where you feel valued, respected, and cherished—and if that's not what you're getting, it's perfectly okay to walk away. In fact, it's the bravest thing you can do.

So, if you find yourself stuck in a relationship that's causing you more pain than joy, take a deep breath and remind yourself that it's okay to let go. It's okay to say goodbye to something that no longer serves you, and it's okay to choose yourself, even if it means walking away from someone you care about.

And remember, letting go doesn't mean you're giving up or admitting defeat. It means you're choosing to prioritize your own well-being and happiness, and that's something worth celebrating. So, take that leap of faith, trust in yourself, and know that brighter days are ahead. You've got this.

It's Okay Not to Be Okay

Can we have a heart-to-heart for a moment? Because I want you to know something—it's okay not to be okay. Seriously, it's more than okay—it's perfectly normal, human, and downright essential. So, let's dive into why it's okay not to be okay and how you can navigate these stormy waters with grace and resilience.

First things first—acknowledging your pain. This is a biggie. It's like shining a spotlight on the dark corners of your soul and saying, "Hey, I see you, and I'm not afraid to face you head-on." So, how do you do it? Step one: give yourself permission to feel. That's right—give yourself a big, fat permission slip to feel whatever it is you're feeling—whether it's sadness, anger, fear, or confusion. And trust me, it's okay to feel all of it.

Next up, let's talk about feeling your feelings. This might sound simple, but trust me, it's anything but. We live in a society that often encourages us to sweep our emotions under the rug or slap on a happy face, even when we're hurting inside. But feelings are like waves. They come and go, rising and falling with the ebb and flow of life. And trying to suppress them? Well, it's like trying to hold back the tide—eventually, they'll come crashing down with even more force.

So, how do you feel your feelings? It starts with getting curious. Instead of running away from your emotions, lean into them. Get curious about where they're coming from, what triggered them, and what they're trying to tell you. And remember, it's okay to sit with your feelings, even when they're uncomfortable. In fact, that discomfort is often a sign that you're on the right track.

Now, let's talk about processing anger—with your ex and with yourself. Anger is a tricky emotion. It's like a wildfire, burning hot and fast, consuming everything in its path. But anger is also a messenger, telling us when our boundaries have been violated or our needs have been ignored. So, how do you process anger in a healthy way?

Let's start with your ex. First off, it's okay to be angry.

Heck, it's more than okay—it's totally understandable. But instead of lashing out or seeking revenge, try channeling that anger into something productive. Write a letter (that you'll never send), scream into a pillow, or punch a punching bag—whatever helps you release that pent-up energy in a safe and constructive way.

Now, let's talk about processing anger with yourself. This one's a toughie, I know. It's easy to beat yourself up, to second-guess your decisions, and to wallow in a sea of self-blame. But nobody's perfect. We all make mistakes, we all screw up, and we all have moments we're not proud of. And that's okay.

So, how do you process anger with yourself? It starts with self-compassion. Treat yourself with the same kindness and understanding you'd show a friend who's going through a tough time. Acknowledge your mistakes, learn from them, and then let them go. And remember, forgiveness isn't about excusing bad behavior; it's about freeing yourself from the burden of resentment and moving forward with grace.

In the end, remember this—it's okay not to be okay. It's okay to feel your feelings, to acknowledge your pain, and to process your anger in a healthy and constructive way. And most importantly, it's okay to ask for help if you need it. Whether it's talking to a trusted friend, journaling your thoughts, or seeking support from a therapist, there's no shame in reaching out for support when you need it most. You've got this.

How to Keep Yourself From Coming Back

Can I let you in on a little secret? Wanting to get back together with your ex after a breakup? Yeah, it's about as common as a rainy day in April. Seriously, you're not alone in feeling this way. But here's the thing—just because the desire is there doesn't mean it's good for you. In fact, sticking to zero contact and resisting the urge to go back is crucial for your healing and growth. So, let's talk about how to do just that.

First off, let's acknowledge the elephant in the room— the temptation to get back together. It's like a siren song, luring you back into the familiar arms of your ex with promises of comfort, familiarity, and security. And trust me, I get it—breaking up is hard, and the idea of going back to what's comfortable can be incredibly tempting. But here's the reality check—going back won't magically fix things. In fact, it'll likely just prolong your pain and delay your healing.

So, how do you keep yourself from coming back? Step one: Establish and maintain zero contact. That means no calls, no texts, no social media stalking—nada. It might sting at first, but trust me, it's the best thing you can do for yourself right now. Cutting off all communication gives you the space and clarity you need to heal, grow, and move forward with your life.

Next up, let's talk about setting boundaries. This is a biggie. Establishing clear boundaries with your ex—and sticking to them—is key to maintaining zero contact and protecting your emotional well-being. Whether it's blocking their number, unfollowing them on social media, or avoiding places where you're likely to run into them, do whatever it takes to create a healthy distance between you.

Now, let's talk about staying strong when the urge to reach out hits. Believe me, it will hit—probably when you least expect it and least want it to. But here's the thing— you're stronger than you think. Instead of giving in to the temptation to contact your ex, try reaching out to a friend or family member instead. Call up your bestie for a coffee date, vent to your mom over the phone, or go for a long walk and let your thoughts wander. Whatever you do, just remember —you've got a whole army of people in your corner cheering you on, and you don't need your ex to validate your worth.

And let's not forget about self-care. This is non-negotiable. Breakups are tough, and they take a toll on both your physical and emotional well-being. So, make self-care a top priority. Whether it's hitting the gym, indulging in a bubble bath, or binge-watching your favorite TV show, do whatever brings you comfort and joy. And remember, taking care of yourself isn't selfish—it's essential.

Finally, let's talk about staying focused on the bigger picture. It's easy to get caught up in the whirlwind of emotions that come with a breakup, but try to keep your eye on the prize—your own happiness and well-being. Remember, letting go of what's familiar is scary, but it's also necessary for growth. By staying true to yourself and honoring your own needs, you're paving the way for a brighter, happier future—one that's free from the chains of the past.

In the end, don't forget that you deserve to be in a relationship that brings you joy, fulfillment, and mutual respect. And if your ex isn't able to provide that for you, then it's okay to let go and move on. Stay strong, stay focused, and know that brighter days are ahead.

Writing the Hurt Away

Ready to pick up your pen and start writing your way to healing? Let's dive into the wonderful world of journaling— a powerful tool for processing emotions, gaining clarity, and finding solace in the midst of chaos. And guess what? You don't need to be a seasoned writer or have perfect grammar to reap the benefits of journaling. All you need is an open heart and a willingness to put pen to paper. So, let's get started.

How to Start a Journaling Habit

Step 1: Choose Your Tools

Grab a journal that speaks to your soul—whether it's a sleek leather-bound notebook or a colorful spiral-bound pad, find something that inspires you to pour your heart out onto the page. And don't forget your favorite pen—the one that glides effortlessly across the paper and makes your handwriting look like a work of art.

Step 2: Set the Scene

Create a cozy, inviting space where you can journal without distractions. Light a candle, play some soothing music, or brew a cup of your favorite tea—whatever helps you feel relaxed and centered.

Step 3: Pick a Time

Choose a consistent time each day to journal—whether it's first thing in the morning, during your lunch break, or right before bed. Consistency is key when it comes to forming a journaling habit, so stick to your chosen time as much as possible.

Step 4: Start Small

Don't overwhelm yourself with the pressure to write a novel every time you sit down to journal. Start with just a few minutes each day and gradually increase the length of your writing sessions as you become more comfortable.

Step 5: Write Freely

There are no rules when it comes to journaling—no right or wrong way to do it. Let your thoughts flow freely onto the page, without censoring or judging yourself. This is your safe space to express yourself honestly and authentically.

Journal Prompts

1. What are you feeling right now, in this moment?
2. What is one thing you're grateful for today?
3. Describe a recent challenge you've faced and how it made you feel.
4. Write a letter to your past self, offering words of encouragement and wisdom.
5. List three things that bring you joy and why.
6. Reflect on a recent accomplishment and how it made you feel.
7. What are three things you can do to practice self-care today?
8. Describe a difficult conversation you need to have and how you plan to approach it.
9. Write about a fear you've been holding onto and why it's been holding you back.
10. What are three things you love about yourself and why?
11. Reflect on a mistake you've made and what you've learned from it.
12. Describe a recent moment of pure happiness and how it made you feel.
13. Write about a goal you're working toward and why it's important to you.

14. List five things you need to let go of in order to move forward.

15. Reflect on a relationship that's been challenging and what you've learned from it.

16. Describe a recent disappointment and how you're choosing to respond.

17. Write a letter to someone who has hurt you, expressing your feelings and seeking closure.

18. List three things you're proud of accomplishing this week.

19. Reflect on a time when you felt completely overwhelmed and how you managed to get through it.

20. Write about a dream or aspiration you have for the future and what steps you can take to make it a reality.

Remember, journaling is a deeply personal practice—there's no right or wrong way to do it. Trust yourself, follow your intuition, and allow the words to flow from your heart onto the page. You've got this.

As you courageously acknowledge the raw emotions that linger after heartbreak and recognize the necessity of letting go, you pave the way for the next chapter—a profound exploration of forgiveness. In the journey ahead, we delve into the transformative power of embracing forgiveness, the crucial step of releasing false hope, and the cathartic process of genuine grieving, all leading you toward a path of profound healing and self-discovery. So, grab your journal, light a candle, and get ready to embark on a journey of forgiveness, growth, and transformation. Trust me, the best is yet to come.

2

E—EMBRACE FORGIVENESS

Forgiving isn't something you do for someone else. It's something you do for yourself. It's saying, 'You're not important enough to have a stranglehold on me.' It's saying, 'You don't get to trap me in the past. I am worthy of a future'

— JODI PICOULT

P icture this: You're standing at a crossroads, weighed down by the burden of resentment and bitterness. In one direction lies the past, a tangled web of hurt and betrayal. In the other lies the future, a path of healing, growth, and possibility. Which way do you choose?

This chapter is all about embracing forgiveness—not for the sake of others, but for your own well-being.

We'll explore the transformative power of forgiveness, the importance of letting go of false hope, and the healing process of proper grieving. It's about releasing the weight of resentment, acknowledging the reality of the end, and allowing yourself the space to grieve. Because forgiveness isn't about absolving others of their mistakes; it's about freeing yourself from the chains of anger and bitterness.

It won't be easy, but trust me—the journey ahead is worth every tear, every moment of discomfort. Because on the other side lies the promise of genuine healing and the possibility of new, healthier beginnings. Let's do this together.

Why We Must First and Foremost Forgive

Alright, let's dive into the deep end of the forgiveness pool, shall we? Because forgiveness is not just a nice-to-have. It's a must-have. And trust me when I say that the power of forgiveness in the healing process is nothing short of miraculous.

Think of forgiveness as a key—a key that unlocks the door to your heart, allowing love, healing, and peace to flood in. Are you holding onto anger, resentment, and bitterness? It's like locking that door tight, trapping yourself in a prison of your own making. So, why must we first and foremost forgive? Let me break it down for you.

First off, forgiveness is like a magic wand, transforming pain into power. When we forgive, we reclaim our agency, refusing to let the actions of others dictate our emotional state. Responding to hate, anger, or mistreatment with kindness, love, and compassion? Yeah, it's probably one of the most difficult things we can be asked to do. But it's also one of the most liberating.

Picture this: You're seething with anger, consumed by thoughts of revenge, imagining all the ways you could make the person who hurt you pay for their actions. But harboring that anger and resentment? It doesn't actually hurt them. In fact, it does them no harm whatsoever in the way that you would like. It's like trying to fight fire with fire —all it does is fuel the flames, leaving you both scorched and wounded.

When you realize that your anger isn't serving its intended purpose—that it's not actually hurting the person who hurt you—it's like flipping a switch in your brain. Suddenly, revenge doesn't seem so appealing. Instead, you start to shift your focus from retaliation to redemption. You begin to see that holding onto anger only keeps you trapped in a cycle of pain and suffering, while forgiveness offers the promise of freedom and healing.

And let me tell you, leading a happy and fulfilling life where you feel free of the burdens of anger? That's the ultimate revenge. It's like sticking it to the universe, saying, "You thought you could break me, but look at me now—I'm thriving." It's about reclaiming your power, refusing to let the actions of others dictate your happiness or well-being.

So, the next time you find yourself consumed by thoughts of revenge, take a step back and ask yourself: Is this anger serving me? Is it bringing me closer to healing and peace? Chances are, the answer is no. And that's when you know it's time to let go, to forgive, and to focus on building a life that's filled with love, joy, and fulfillment. Because in the end, that's the sweetest revenge of all.

But forgiveness isn't just about letting go of the past. It's about embracing the future with open arms. It's about seeing the negative experiences as opportunities for growth and transformation. Because when we hold onto anger and resentment, we're not hurting the other person—we're hurting ourselves.

So, how do we go about forgiving others for what they've

done? It starts with kindness, compassion, and empathy—not just toward others, but toward ourselves as well—giving ourselves permission to heal, grow, and develop at our own pace. And what about retraining your way of thinking? It's like flexing a muscle—the more you practice, the stronger you become.

Stop telling the story of how you were hurt from your perspective and imagine it from the perspective of the person who has hurt you. It's a game-changer. It's like stepping into their shoes, seeing the world through their eyes, and realizing that hurt people hurt people. And you know what? It's okay to send them positive thoughts instead of ones filled with anger and resentment. It's not about condoning their actions; it's about setting yourself free.

In the end, forgiveness isn't just a gift we give to others; it's a gift we give to ourselves. So, grab that magic wand, unlock the door to your heart, and let the healing begin.

Why It Isn't Easy to Forgive

We've all heard the saying, "Forgive and forget," but let's be real here—forgiveness? Yeah, it's often easier said than done. Especially when the one who hurt us is someone we love, someone we trusted with our heart and soul. So, why is forgiveness so difficult? Let's dive into it.

Starting from a young age, we're taught to forgive people because it's "the right thing to do." But here's the thing—what's right isn't always what's easy. Sometimes, it's the most difficult path to take. And you know what? That's okay. Forgiveness isn't a one-size-fits-all solution. It's messy, complicated, and downright hard sometimes. But trust me when I say that it's worth it.

So, let's break it down, shall we? Here are five reasons why forgiveness is often so darn difficult:

Language gives us the ability to hold onto memories longer

Ever find yourself replaying a past hurt over and over again in your mind? Yeah, blame it on language. According to physicist Frank Heile, our ability to think and communicate in language keeps us stuck in the past, unable to let go of painful memories (5 Reasons Why It's Hard to Forgive People, n.d.). It's like we're trapped in a time machine, constantly reliving our hurts and resentments. No wonder forgiveness feels like an uphill battle.

There's too much anger that causes a lack of self-control

Anger can be a powerful emotion, clouding our judgment and making forgiveness feel impossible. When we're consumed by anger, it's hard to see past our own hurt and resentment. We may even use anger as a defense mechanism, justifying our refusal to forgive as a way to protect ourselves. But here's the thing—forgiveness requires empathy, understanding, and a willingness to let go of our anger.

You may be scared to forgive, in fear of getting hurt again.

Let's face it—getting hurt sucks. And when we've been hurt in the past, it's natural to be wary of opening ourselves up to the possibility of being hurt again. So, we build walls around our hearts, shutting out the possibility of forgiveness in order to protect ourselves from further pain. But here's the thing—forgiveness isn't about letting the other person off the hook; it's about setting yourself free.

You may believe that the person who offended you deserves punishment.

Holding a grudge can feel empowering, like we're taking back control after being wronged. But here's the reality check—holding onto resentment only hurts us in the long run. It's like carrying around a heavy burden, while the other person moves on with their life. And let me tell you, that's not a burden worth bearing.

You feel misunderstood and find it hard to trust or let the offensive party in.

Ever feel like the person who hurt you just doesn't get it? Yeah, that's a tough pill to swallow. It's hard to forgive someone when they've never made you feel understood or heard. But here's the thing—forgiveness isn't about letting the other person off the hook; it's about setting yourself free.

So, there you have it—five reasons why forgiveness is often so darn difficult. But it's not impossible. With time, patience, and a whole lot of self-love, forgiveness is within reach. So, take a deep breath, my friend, and remember— you're stronger than you think. And you deserve to be free from the burdens of anger and resentment.

Forgiving Yourself

Trust me when I say that forgiving yourself might just be the hardest forgiveness journey you'll ever embark on. But guess what? You're not alone. We've all been there, beating ourselves up over past mistakes and wishing we could turn back the clock. So, how do you truly forgive yourself for allowing yourself to be in the situation you're in? Let's break it down.

First things first, let's get one thing straight—self-forgiveness is not about letting yourself off the hook, nor is it a sign of weakness. It's about acknowledging your humanity, accepting your flaws, and giving yourself the grace to grow and evolve. So, let's dive into the 4 R's of self-forgiveness and explore how you can start your journey toward healing and self-compassion (Cherry, 2023).

1. **Responsibility:** Take ownership of your actions and their consequences. Understand that while you may not have intended to cause harm, your choices led to certain outcomes. It's about facing the truth head-on, without making excuses or shifting blame onto others. Remember, accepting responsibility is the first step toward growth and transformation.

2. **Remorse:** Allow yourself to feel the weight of your mistakes. Express genuine remorse for the pain you may have caused yourself and others. This isn't about wallowing in guilt or self-pity; it's about acknowledging the impact of your actions and showing empathy toward those you've hurt. Remember, remorse is a powerful catalyst for change.

3. **Restoration:** Treat yourself with kindness and compassion. Offer yourself the same level of forgiveness and understanding that you would offer to a friend in a similar situation. Practice self-care, engage in activities that bring you joy,

and surround yourself with supportive people
who lift you up. Remember, you deserve love and
forgiveness—from others and from yourself.

4. **Renewal:** Focus on growth and transformation.
   Look for ways to learn from your mistakes and
   make better choices in the future. Use your past
   experiences as stepping stones toward a brighter,
   more fulfilling future. Remember, every setback
   is an opportunity for growth, and every mistake
   is a lesson in disguise.

Now, let's put these 4 R's into action, shall we? Here's
how you can truly forgive yourself and start afresh:

- **Understand your emotions:** Allow yourself to
  feel whatever emotions come up—whether it's
  guilt, shame, or regret. Remember, emotions are
  a natural part of the healing process, so don't be
  afraid to lean into them.
- **Accept responsibility for what happened:** Own
  up to your mistakes and their consequences.
  Avoid making excuses or blaming others for your
  actions. Remember, true accountability is the key
  to personal growth and transformation.
- **Treat yourself with kindness and compassion:**
  Be gentle with yourself, especially during
  difficult times. Practice self-care, engage in
  activities that nourish your soul, and surround
  yourself with people who uplift and support you.
- **Express remorse for your mistakes:** Apologize
  to yourself and to anyone you may have hurt
  along the way. Be sincere in your apology and
  strive to make amends wherever possible.

Remember, genuine remorse is a powerful catalyst for healing and reconciliation.

- **Make amends and apologize (including apologizing to yourself):** Take proactive steps to make things right, whether it's through restitution, reconciliation, or simply offering a heartfelt apology. Remember, actions speak louder than words, so let your actions reflect your commitment to change.

- **Look for ways to learn from the experience:** Use your past mistakes as learning opportunities. Reflect on what went wrong and how you can avoid similar pitfalls in the future. Remember, every setback is a chance to grow stronger and wiser.

- **Focus on making better choices in the future:** Commit to living a life aligned with your values and aspirations. Set goals, make plans, and take proactive steps toward a brighter, more fulfilling future. Remember, forgiveness isn't just about letting go of the past; it's about embracing the possibilities of the future.

In the end, self-forgiveness is about embracing your humanity, accepting your imperfections, and giving yourself the grace to grow and evolve. So, be patient with yourself, my friend, and remember—you are worthy of love, forgiveness, and redemption.

Forgive the One Who Broke Your Heart

Forgiving the one who broke your heart? Yeah, I know—it sounds like mission impossible. But trust me when I say that it's not only possible but also incredibly liberating. So, how do you open your heart to forgive someone who has caused you so much pain? Let's explore some ways to navigate this challenging journey.

- **Acknowledge your feelings:** Before you can even begin to think about forgiveness, it's essential to acknowledge and validate your feelings. Allow yourself to feel whatever emotions come up—whether it's anger, sadness, betrayal, or even indifference. Remember, your feelings are valid, and it's okay to give yourself permission to feel them.
- **Practice empathy:** Put yourself in the other person's shoes and try to understand their perspective. While this doesn't mean excusing or justifying their actions, it does help humanize them and foster empathy. Recognize that hurt people hurt people, and the person who hurt you may have been dealing with their pain and insecurities.
- **Release resentment:** Holding onto resentment only keeps you tethered to the past, preventing you from moving forward. Practice letting go of resentment by consciously choosing to release the grip it has on your heart. This doesn't mean forgetting or condoning what happened; it simply means freeing yourself from the burden of bitterness.
- **Set boundaries:** Forgiveness doesn't mean letting the other person back into your life or subjecting yourself to further harm. It's crucial to set healthy boundaries to protect yourself and

prioritize your well-being. This may involve limiting or cutting off contact with the person who hurt you, at least until you feel ready to engage with them again.

- **Focus on healing:** Redirect your energy toward your own healing and growth. Engage in activities that bring you joy, spend time with supportive friends and family, and prioritize self-care. Remember, forgiveness is as much about healing yourself as it is about letting go of resentment toward others.
- **Practice self-compassion:** Be kind and compassionate toward yourself throughout this process. Remember that forgiveness isn't about letting the other person off the hook; it's about setting yourself free. Give yourself permission to feel your emotions, make mistakes, and take the time you need to heal.
- **Practice mindfulness:** Cultivate mindfulness and present-moment awareness to help you stay grounded and centered amidst difficult emotions. Practice mindfulness techniques such as deep breathing, meditation, or yoga to help you navigate the ups and downs of the forgiveness journey with greater ease and clarity.
- **Seek support:** Don't be afraid to reach out for support from friends, family, or a therapist. Talking to someone who can offer empathy, validation, and perspective can be incredibly helpful as you navigate the complexities of forgiveness.
- **Release expectations:** Let go of any expectations you may have about how the other person

should respond to your forgiveness. Remember, forgiveness is ultimately about freeing yourself from the burden of resentment—it's not dependent on the other person's actions or reactions.

In the end, forgiveness is a deeply personal journey—one that takes time, patience, and courage. But trust me when I say that it's worth it. By opening your heart to forgiveness, you reclaim your power, liberate yourself from the shackles of resentment, and pave the way for healing and growth. So, take a deep breath, my friend, and remember—you are stronger and more resilient than you think.

Letting Go of False Hope

Clinging onto unrealistic expectations can be like holding onto a sinking ship. It's time to let go of those rose-tinted glasses and face the cold, hard truth. So, buckle up, because we're diving deep into the dangers of false hope and how to break free from its grip.

The Danger of False Hope

First things first, let's talk about why false hope can be so darn dangerous. Picture this—you're holding onto the belief that somehow, someday, things will magically fall back into place. Maybe it's wishful thinking, maybe it's denial, but either way, it's keeping you stuck in a state of limbo. You're putting your life on hold, waiting for a miracle that may never come.

But here's the reality check—clinging onto false hope

only prolongs your pain and delays your healing. It's like chasing after a mirage in the desert, hoping to quench your thirst with something that doesn't even exist. And let me tell you, the longer you chase after that illusion, the further you stray from the path of true healing and growth.

Ways to Let Go of False Hope

So, how do you break free from the clutches of false hope? Here are a few strategies to help you let go and move forward with clarity and courage:

- **Face the truth:** The first step toward letting go of false hope is to face the truth head-on. Take a long, hard look at the reality of your situation— the good, the bad, and the ugly. Acknowledge that the relationship is over, and that clinging onto false hope will only prolong your pain.
- **Set realistic expectations:** It's time to let go of the fairy tale ending and embrace reality. Accept that things may never go back to the way they were, and that's okay. Instead of chasing after unrealistic fantasies, focus on building a future based on truth and authenticity.
- **Practice acceptance:** Acceptance doesn't mean giving up or surrendering to despair. Rather, it's about acknowledging the reality of your situation and finding peace within it. Embrace the uncertainty of the future, and trust that better things are on the horizon.
- **Focus on self-improvement:** Instead of pinning all your hopes on mending the relationship, shift your focus inward and focus on self-

improvement. Invest in your own growth and development, and strive to become the best version of yourself. Remember, true happiness comes from within, not from external sources.

- **Surround yourself with support:** Surround yourself with people who uplift and support you on your journey toward healing. Lean on friends, family, or support groups who understand what you're going through and can offer guidance and encouragement.

- **Practice mindfulness:** Stay grounded in the present moment and cultivate mindfulness in your daily life. Practice techniques such as deep breathing, meditation, or journaling to help quiet your mind and find inner peace.

- **Set boundaries:** It's important to set healthy boundaries to protect yourself from falling back into the trap of false hope. Communicate your needs and expectations clearly, and be prepared to enforce those boundaries if necessary.

- **Seek professional help:** If you're struggling to let go of false hope on your own, don't hesitate to seek professional help. A therapist or counselor can provide valuable guidance and support as you navigate the complexities of healing from heartbreak.

In the end, letting go of false hope is a process—not an event. It takes time, patience, and a whole lot of self-love. But the freedom you'll find on the other side is worth every ounce of effort. So, take a deep breath, my friend, and take that first step toward true healing and liberation.

Grieving the End of a Relationship

When a relationship comes to an end, it's like a storm raging inside us, tearing apart the very fabric of our being. But amidst the chaos, there's a glimmer of hope—the promise of healing and renewal. So, let's navigate through the stages of relationship grief and explore how to navigate this tumultuous journey toward healing.

Stages of Relationship Grief

Dr. Elisabeth Kübler-Ross famously outlined the stages of grief, originally applied to the process of mourning death (Kromberg, 2013). However, these stages also resonate deeply with the experience of a breakup. Let's break them down:

Denial

In this initial phase, denial takes the wheel as we grapple with the reality of life without our significant other. Despite knowing deep down that the relationship is over, we cling to fleeting hopes and fantasies of reconciliation. It's like trying to convince ourselves that the sky isn't really falling, even as the ground crumbles beneath our feet. Late-night texts and lingering glimmers of hope become our companions in this surreal dance of denial.

Anger

Next up, anger comes crashing in like a tidal wave, sweeping away any semblance of peace or acceptance. We direct our fury at our ex-partner, at the universe, at anyone

and anything associated with the breakup. It's a whirlwind
of blame and bitterness, fueled by the searing pain of
betrayal and loss. We lash out, we vent, we seek solace in the
catharsis of rage—but deep down, we know that beneath
the anger lies a wellspring of hurt.

Bargaining

Bargaining often goes hand in hand with denial, as we
desperately seek loopholes in the fabric of fate. We make
grand promises and empty threats in a desperate bid to salvage
what remains of the relationship. We plead with our ex, we
bargain with the universe, we grasp at straws in a futile attempt
to rewrite the script of our lives. But no amount of negotiation
or magical thinking can turn back the hands of time.

Depression

Ah, depression—the heavy blanket of sadness that
threatens to smother us in its suffocating embrace. It's the
weight of hopelessness bearing down on our weary shoulders, the relentless ache of grief echoing in the depths of our
soul. We retreat into ourselves, withdrawing from the world
as we drown in a sea of tears and despair. It's a dark and
lonely place, but amidst the shadows, there's a glimmer of
acceptance waiting to be found.

Acceptance

Finally, acceptance beckons like a distant beacon of
light, guiding us toward the shores of peace and closure. It's
not a sudden epiphany, but rather a gradual surrender to

the inevitability of change. We make peace with the loss, we let go of the past, and we slowly but surely begin to rebuild our lives from the ashes of our pain. There's still sadness, still longing, but beneath it all lies a newfound sense of strength and resilience.

How to Grieve the End of a Relationship

Now that we've mapped out the stages of grief, let's explore some practical strategies for navigating this tumultuous journey toward healing:

- **Spend time 'introverting':** Take this opportunity to reconnect with yourself and your passions. Embrace solitude as a chance to reflect, create, and rejuvenate. Dive into your hobbies, rediscover forgotten interests, and use this time alone to nurture your soul.
- **Do what you want without compromise:** Reclaim your autonomy and indulge in the things that bring you joy. Rediscover your personal preferences and habits, free from the constraints of compromise. Whether it's binge-watching your favorite shows or wandering aimlessly through the aisles of Target, prioritize your own happiness.
- **Share your feelings with your support system:** Don't bottle up your emotions—let them out, loud and clear. Lean on your support system, whether it's friends, family, or a therapist, and allow yourself to express your sadness, anger, and frustration. Give yourself permission to cry,

to scream, to dance it out—whatever helps you release the pent-up emotions inside.

- **Boost your self-esteem:** A breakup can take a toll on your self-esteem, so take this time to rebuild and reaffirm your sense of self-worth. Engage in activities that make you feel good about yourself, whether it's hitting the gym, pursuing a passion project, or simply practicing self-care.

- **Reconnect with your authentic self:** Use this period of introspection to rediscover what makes you unique and special. Reconnect with the qualities and interests that make you who you are, and embrace the fullness of your individuality. Celebrate your strengths, acknowledge your vulnerabilities, and remember that you are worthy of love and happiness.

- **Notice your emotional reactivity:** Pay attention to your emotional responses when thoughts of your ex arise. Notice any patterns of reactivity, and strive for moments of acceptance rather than dwelling in pain. Allow yourself to acknowledge both the good and the bad aspects of the relationship, and recognize your inherent worthiness of a fulfilling future.

In the end, grieving the end of a relationship is a deeply personal journey—there's no one-size-fits-all approach. But by embracing the stages of grief, practicing self-compassion, and surrounding yourself with love and support, you can navigate this challenging terrain with grace and resilience. Remember, dear friend, that healing is not a destination but a journey—and you are stronger and more resilient than you know.

Writing a Letter You'll Never Send

There's something inherently liberating about pouring your heart out onto paper, knowing that your words will remain unseen by their intended recipient. It's a sacred space for raw honesty and unfiltered expression, free from the constraints of judgment or expectation. Writing a letter you'll never send allows you to confront your feelings head-on, without the fear of repercussions or rejection. It's a form of self-expression that honors your truth and validates your experience, regardless of whether or not it's ever acknowledged by the other person.

Moreover, writing can be a form of release—a way to untangle the knots of emotion that have been weighing heavy on your heart. By externalizing your thoughts and feelings through written words, you create distance between yourself and the pain, allowing for a sense of clarity and perspective to emerge. It's a cathartic process of purging the pent-up emotions that have been festering within, making space for healing and renewal to take root.

Instructions and Tips

Now that we've explored the why let's dive into the how. Here are some instructions and tips to help you craft a letter you'll never send:

- Create a calm and peaceful environment where you can fully immerse yourself in the writing process. Settle into a comfortable spot, free from distractions, and allow yourself to sink into the depths of your emotions.

- Before you begin writing, take a moment to set intentions for your letter. What do you hope to achieve through this process? Is it closure, understanding, or simply a release of pent-up emotions? Clarifying your intentions will guide your writing and help you stay focused on your goals.

- Begin your letter with a note of gratitude—not necessarily for the person themselves, but for the lessons and experiences they've brought into your life. Expressing gratitude can help shift your perspective from bitterness to appreciation, allowing you to find silver linings amidst the pain.

- Be honest and authentic in your writing, allowing yourself to express the full spectrum of your emotions. Whether it's anger, sadness, regret, or longing, give yourself permission to let it all out without censorship or judgment. Remember, this letter is for your eyes only—so don't hold back.

- While it's natural to assign blame or point fingers in the aftermath of a breakup, try to steer clear of accusatory language in your letter. Instead, focus on expressing your own feelings and experiences without casting judgment on the other person. This is your opportunity to take ownership of your emotions, rather than assigning fault to someone else.

- Let go of any expectations or attachments to how the other person will receive or respond to your letter. Remember, the purpose of writing a letter you'll never send is not to elicit a reaction from the other person but to find closure and healing within yourself. Release the need for validation or closure from external sources, and trust in the power of your own healing journey.

- There are various types of letters you can write, depending on your intentions and the nature of your relationship. Some examples include:
- **A letter of closure:** Expressing your final thoughts and feelings, and officially closing the chapter on your relationship.
- **A letter of forgiveness:** Extending forgiveness to yourself or the other person, and releasing any lingering resentment or anger.
- **A letter of gratitude:** Reflecting on the positive aspects of your relationship and expressing gratitude for the memories and lessons learned.
- **A letter of apology:** Taking responsibility for any mistakes or hurt caused during the relationship, and expressing genuine remorse.
- **A letter of unsent truths:** Sharing the unspoken truths or feelings that you've been holding back, without fear of judgment or rejection.

Example Letter

Dear [Name],

I'm writing this letter even though I know you'll never read it. It's more for me than for you. There are so many things I wish I could say to you, but I know it's best if I keep them to myself.

I want you to know that I've been thinking a lot about us lately. It's been tough, you know? Remembering all the good times we had, but also the bad ones. I've been feeling a mix of emotions—sadness, anger, confusion.

But I've come to realize that holding onto these feelings isn't doing me any good. It's like carrying around a heavy weight on my shoulders all the time. So, I've decided to let go.

I forgive you for everything that happened between us. I forgive myself too. We're only human, after all, and we all make mistakes.

I want you to be happy, even if that means it's without me. And I hope you can find it in your heart to forgive me too.

So, this is me saying goodbye. Not because I want to, but because I know it's what's best for both of us.

Take care of yourself,

[Your Name]

In wrapping up our journey through the transformative landscape of forgiveness, I want you to remember one thing: It's not just about letting go of the past, but about reclaiming your present and shaping your future. As we navigate the healing power of forgiveness, the next chapter unfolds with a call to action. It's about shifting your focus from the past by engaging in purposeful pursuits, unlocking a world of productivity that not only enriches your life but nurtures your mental well-being. So, let's begin this journey together, embracing every step as we move toward a brighter tomorrow.

3

C—CHANNEL YOUR HEARTBREAK ENERGY

Both good and bad days should end with productivity.
Your mood affairs should never influence your work.

— GREG EVANS

Have you ever felt like your emotions are dictating your productivity? It's a common struggle, but one that we can overcome together. In this chapter, we're diving into the power of channeling your heartbreak energy into something constructive. It's all about refusing to let your emotions hold you back from living a fulfilling life. Instead of succumbing to idleness or despair, let's explore how we can redirect that energy into activities that not only enhance our well-being but also propel us forward on our journey of healing.

The Link Between Depression and Fatigue

It's a cruel reality: not only does heartbreak weigh heavy on your heart, but it can also drag down your energy levels, leaving you feeling utterly exhausted. Have you ever experienced days where simply getting out of bed feels like an insurmountable task? If so, you're not alone. Fatigue is a common companion of depression, with over 90% of individuals experiencing this draining sensation when navigating through the depths of emotional turmoil (Rodriguez, 2021).

When your heart is heavy with sorrow, it's no surprise that your energy reserves take a hit. Depression, with its persistent feelings of sadness, anxiety, and hopelessness, has a knack for sapping away our vitality. But why does depression make us feel so weary? Let's delve into the intricate relationship between depression and fatigue.

For starters, depression can wreak havoc on our sleep patterns. Whether it's struggling to fall asleep or finding yourself lost in the abyss of insomnia, sleep disturbances are a hallmark of depression, affecting around 80% of individuals grappling with this mental health condition (Rodriguez, 2021). And it's not just a lack of sleep that leaves us feeling drained; oversleeping, another common symptom of depression, can also contribute to feelings of exhaustion.

But it's not just our sleep that suffers. Depression can throw a wrench into our eating habits, leading to decreased appetite or an overwhelming desire for sugary, less nutritious foods. These dietary shifts can leave us feeling sluggish and devoid of energy, as our bodies miss out on the vital nutrients found in fruits, vegetables, and whole grains.

Exercise, a natural energy booster, often takes a backseat when depression comes knocking. Despite knowing the benefits of physical activity, feelings of low motivation and reduced self-esteem can hinder our ability to lace up our sneakers and hit the gym. It's not laziness—it's the weight of depression making every step feel like an uphill battle.

And let's not forget about stress. Depression and stress are intertwined, each exacerbating the other in a never-ending cycle of emotional turmoil. The chronic stress brought on by depression can leave us feeling drained and depleted as our overactive amygdala churns out negative thoughts faster than we can keep up.

But fear not for there is hope on the horizon. By understanding the intricate ways in which depression drains our energy, we gain valuable insights into how to combat this fatigue and reclaim our vitality. In the next sections, we'll explore practical strategies for managing depression-induced fatigue, empowering you to take charge of your energy levels and embark on a journey toward renewed vigor and vitality.

How to Overcome Depression Fatigue

If you're feeling weighed down by the heavy fog of depression fatigue, know that you're not alone. Many have trodden this path before you, and while it may seem daunting, there are steps you can take to lighten the load and reclaim your vitality.

- **Prioritize sleep:** Getting quality rest is crucial for replenishing your energy reserves and combating fatigue. Establish a consistent sleep schedule, aiming for 7-9 hours of shut-eye each night. Create a relaxing bedtime routine to signal to your body that it's time to wind down. Limit screen time before bed and create a comfortable sleep environment conducive to restorative slumber.

- **Nourish your body:** Next up, let's nourish that tired body of yours. Depression often messes with our appetite, leading to poor eating habits and nutritional deficiencies. Focus on fueling your body with wholesome, nutrient-rich foods like fruits, vegetables, whole grains, and lean proteins. Stay hydrated by drinking plenty of water throughout the day, and limit your intake of caffeine and sugary snacks, which can cause energy crashes.

- **Get moving:** I know, I know—when you're feeling exhausted, the last thing you want to do is exercise. But trust me, physical activity is one of the best antidotes to fatigue. Start small with gentle activities like walking, yoga, or swimming, and gradually increase the intensity as you build up your stamina. Exercise releases feel-good endorphins that boost your mood and energy levels, making it a powerful tool for combating depression fatigue.

- **Manage stress:** Stress and depression go hand in hand, creating a vicious cycle of exhaustion and emotional turmoil. Take steps to manage stress in your life, whether it's through mindfulness meditation, deep breathing exercises, or engaging in activities that bring you joy and relaxation. Practice self-care rituals like taking soothing baths, spending time in nature, or indulging in your favorite hobbies.

- **Seek support:** You don't have to navigate the murky waters of depression fatigue alone. Reach out to friends, family members, or a trusted therapist for support and guidance. Share your struggles openly and honestly, and don't be afraid to ask for help when you need it. Surround yourself with positive, supportive people who uplift and encourage you on your journey toward healing.

- **Practice self-compassion:** Be gentle with yourself, dear one. Depression fatigue can make even the simplest tasks feel like monumental challenges, and that's okay. Practice self-compassion and kindness toward yourself, acknowledging that you're doing the best you can in difficult circumstances. Celebrate small victories and forgive yourself for setbacks along the way. Remember, healing is a journey, not a destination.

- **Break tasks into manageable steps:** When faced with a mountain of tasks, it's easy to feel overwhelmed and paralyzed by indecision. Break tasks down into smaller, more manageable steps, and tackle them one at a time. Set realistic goals for yourself and celebrate your progress along the way. Remember, even small steps forward are worthy of celebration.

- **Engage in meaningful activities:** Find purpose and meaning in your daily activities by focusing on things that bring you joy, fulfillment, and a sense of accomplishment. Whether it's pursuing a hobby, volunteering in your community, or spending time with loved ones, prioritize activities that nourish your soul and ignite your passion.

- **Practice gratitude:** Cultivate an attitude of gratitude by focusing on the things in your life that you're thankful for, no matter how small. Keep a gratitude journal and write down three things you're grateful for each day. Shifting your perspective toward gratitude can help lift your spirits and boost your energy levels.
- **Be patient and persistent:** Finally, be patient with yourself as you navigate the ups and downs of depression fatigue. Healing takes time, and there will be setbacks along the way. Stay committed to your self-care routine and keep moving forward, one step at a time. Remember, you're stronger than you realize, and brighter days are on the horizon.

So, as you embark on your journey to overcome depression fatigue, remember that you are not defined by your struggles. With courage, resilience, and a dash of self-love, you can conquer fatigue and reclaim your vitality, one small step at a time.

Why Keeping Busy Isn't Entirely a Bad Thing

If you've found yourself diving headfirst into a whirlwind of activities to keep your mind occupied, you're not alone. While keeping busy might seem like a mere distraction from the pain of heartbreak, it actually holds a multitude of surprising benefits for your mental well-being.

Distraction from negative thoughts: Let's start with the most obvious benefit—keeping busy provides a welcome distraction from the incessant chatter of negative thoughts swirling around in your mind. Engaging in activities that require your full attention can help shift your focus away from rumination and self-doubt, giving your weary mind a much-needed break from the pain of heartbreak.

Boost in mood: When you're immersed in activities that bring you joy and fulfillment, your brain releases feel-good chemicals like dopamine and serotonin, which can lift your mood and alleviate feelings of sadness and despair. Whether it's pursuing a hobby, spending time with loved ones, or tackling a challenging project, staying busy can provide a natural mood boost to help combat the blues.

Sense of accomplishment: Accomplishing tasks, no matter how small, can instill a sense of pride and satisfaction that boosts your self-esteem and self-worth. By setting goals and actively working toward achieving them, you reaffirm your ability to overcome obstacles and thrive in the face of adversity. Each small victory serves as a reminder of your resilience and strength, empowering you to tackle even bigger challenges head-on.

Structure and routine: Heartbreak often throws our lives into disarray, leaving us feeling lost and adrift without a sense of purpose or direction. Keeping busy with structured activities and routines can provide much-needed stability and predictability in an otherwise chaotic world. By establishing a daily schedule and sticking to it, you create a sense of order and control that can help anchor you amidst the storm of emotions.

Social connection: Engaging in social activities and spending time with loved ones can provide invaluable support and companionship during times of heartbreak. Whether it's grabbing coffee with a friend, attending a group exercise class, or joining a book club, surrounding yourself with positive and supportive people can help alleviate feelings of loneliness and isolation. Building and nurturing social connections fosters a sense of belonging and community that is essential for emotional well-being.

Expansion of perspective: Keeping busy with new experiences and activities can broaden your perspective and open your mind to new possibilities. Stepping outside of your comfort zone and trying new things exposes you to different people, ideas, and ways of living, helping you grow and evolve as an individual. Embracing novelty and adventure can reignite your zest for life and remind you that there is a world of opportunities waiting to be explored beyond the confines of heartbreak.

Sense of purpose: Engaging in meaningful activities that align with your values and passions can infuse your life with a sense of purpose and meaning. Whether it's volunteering for a cause you believe in, pursuing a creative passion, or making a difference in your community, finding purpose in your actions gives your life direction and significance beyond the pain of heartbreak. Knowing that you are contributing to something greater than yourself can provide a profound sense of fulfillment.

Time for self-reflection: While keeping busy can provide a much-needed distraction from the pain of heartbreak, it's also important to carve out time for self-reflection and introspection. Use moments of solitude to explore your thoughts and feelings, journaling about your experiences, and processing your emotions in a healthy and constructive way. Balancing activity with introspection allows you to gain insight into yourself and your journey toward healing, fostering personal growth and self-awareness along the way.

While keeping busy may not be a cure-all for heartbreak, it can certainly be a powerful tool in your healing arsenal. By staying engaged in activities that bring you joy, fulfillment, and connection, you can boost your mood, enhance your well-being, and navigate the turbulent waters of heartbreak with resilience and grace. So, embrace the busyness of life and let it carry you forward on your journey toward healing and wholeness.

Ways to Keep Moving

Ready to dive into a world of adventure and discovery as we explore some fun and creative ways to keep busy and keep moving forward on our healing journey? Let's dive right in!

- **Explore the great outdoors:** There's nothing quite like the healing power of nature to soothe the soul and lift the spirits. Take a leisurely hike through a scenic trail, go for a bike ride in the countryside, or simply sit and bask in the beauty of a tranquil park. Connecting with the natural world can provide a much-needed escape from the hustle and bustle of everyday life and offer a sense of peace and serenity amidst the chaos of heartbreak.
- **Get crafty:** Unleash your inner artist and get creative with some DIY crafts! Whether it's painting, knitting, scrapbooking, or pottery, immersing yourself in a hands-on creative project can be incredibly therapeutic and rewarding. Plus, you'll have a tangible reminder of your creativity and resilience to cherish long after the pain of heartbreak has faded.
- **Dance like nobody's watching:** Turn up the music and dance your heart out! Whether you

prefer a solo dance party in the comfort of your own home or hitting the dance floor with friends, dancing is a fantastic way to release pent-up emotions, boost your mood, and let loose. So put on your favorite tunes, let go of your inhibitions, and dance away the pain of heartbreak one beat at a time.

- **Volunteer your time:** Giving back to others in need is not only a powerful way to make a positive impact on the world but also to gain perspective and gratitude for your own blessings. Whether it's volunteering at a local soup kitchen, animal shelter, or community garden, lending a helping hand to those less fortunate can bring a sense of purpose and fulfillment to your life and remind you that you are not alone in your struggles.

- **Try something new:** Step outside of your comfort zone and embrace the thrill of new experiences! Whether it's learning a new language, trying a new cuisine, or taking up a new hobby, exploring unfamiliar territory can reignite your passion for life and remind you that there is a world of possibilities waiting to be discovered beyond the confines of heartbreak. So go ahead, take that cooking class, sign up for that dance workshop, or embark on that solo travel adventure—you never know what amazing adventures await!

- **Dive into books:** Escape into the magical world of literature and lose yourself in the pages of a good book. Whether you prefer fiction, non-fiction, or self-help, reading is a fantastic way to expand your horizons, gain new perspectives, and find solace in the written word. So curl up with a cozy blanket, brew a cup of tea, and let the power of storytelling transport you to faraway lands and distant galaxies as you embark on an epic literary journey of healing and self-discovery.

- **Cultivate your green thumb:** Discover the joy of gardening and cultivate your own little oasis of tranquility and beauty. Whether you have a sprawling backyard or just a few pots on a sunny windowsill, growing plants and flowers can be incredibly therapeutic and rewarding. Plus, there's nothing quite like the satisfaction of watching your efforts bloom and flourish before your eyes—a tangible reminder that growth and renewal are possible even in the wake of heartbreak.

- **Connect with your inner child:** Reconnect with the simple joys of childhood and indulge in some playful activities that ignite your sense of wonder and imagination. Whether it's flying a kite, building a sandcastle, or playing a game of tag in the park, tapping into your inner child can help you rediscover the magic and spontaneity of life and bring a smile to your face even on the darkest of days.

Remember, healing from heartbreak is a journey, not a destination. By embracing new experiences, exploring your passions, and staying busy with activities that bring you joy and fulfillment, you're taking important steps toward healing and reclaiming your sense of self.

Planning Ahead

Let's dive into the wonderful world of planning ahead and discover how it can be a powerful tool for nurturing our mental well-being amidst the challenges of heartbreak.

The Benefits of Making Plans

Planning ahead isn't just about filling up your calendar with appointments and commitments—it's about taking control of your life and actively shaping your future in a way that brings you joy, purpose, and fulfillment. Here are some ways in which making plans can benefit your mental health:

- **Sense of purpose and direction:** When you have a clear plan in place, whether it's for the day, week, or month ahead, you give yourself a sense of purpose and direction. Knowing what you want to accomplish and how you're going to do it can help alleviate feelings of aimlessness and uncertainty, giving you a roadmap to follow as you navigate the challenges of heartbreak.
- **Focus and motivation:** Having concrete goals and objectives can provide you with the focus and motivation you need to keep moving forward, even when times get tough. By breaking down your larger goals into smaller, actionable steps, you can create a sense of momentum and progress that fuels your determination to overcome obstacles and achieve success.
- **Sense of control:** Heartbreak can often leave us feeling powerless and out of control, but making plans allows us to reclaim a sense of agency over our lives. By taking proactive steps to shape our future and create positive change, we can regain

a sense of control and autonomy that empowers
us to face the challenges ahead with confidence
and resilience.

- **Reduced anxiety and stress:** When you have a
  plan in place, you can alleviate anxiety and stress
  by eliminating uncertainty and ambiguity.
  Knowing what to expect and having a roadmap
  for how to deal with potential challenges can
  help you feel more prepared and capable of
  handling whatever comes your way, reducing
  feelings of overwhelm and anxiety in the
  process.
- **Increased productivity and satisfaction:** By
  setting goals and making plans to achieve them,
  you can increase your productivity and sense of
  accomplishment. As you check items off your to-
  do list and make progress toward your objectives,
  you'll experience a greater sense of satisfaction
  and fulfillment, boosting your mood and self-
  esteem in the process.

Now that we've explored some of the benefits of making
plans, let's dive into the nitty-gritty of how to actually go
about it.

How to Make Plans

1. **Set clear goals:** Start by identifying what you
   want to achieve and setting clear, actionable
   goals for yourself. Whether it's completing a
   project, pursuing a hobby, or improving your
   mental and emotional well-being, having specific

objectives in mind will help guide your planning process.

2. **Break it down:** Once you've established your goals, break them down into smaller, more manageable tasks or steps. This will make them feel less overwhelming and more achievable, allowing you to make steady progress toward your larger objectives.

3. **Prioritize:** Determine which tasks or activities are most important or urgent, and prioritize them accordingly. Focus on tackling high-priority items first, and then work your way down the list. This will help ensure that you're making the most efficient use of your time and energy.

4. **Create a schedule:** Once you've identified your goals and priorities, create a schedule or timetable for yourself to help you stay on track. Whether you prefer to use a physical planner, a digital calendar, or a smartphone app, find a system that works for you and stick to it.

5. **Be flexible:** While it's important to have a plan in place, it's also essential to remain flexible and adaptable in the face of unexpected challenges or changes. Life doesn't always go according to plan, and that's okay! Be willing to adjust your plans as needed and embrace the opportunity to learn and grow along the way.

6. **Celebrate progress:** As you work toward your goals and make progress, be sure to celebrate your accomplishments along the way. Whether it's treating yourself to a small reward, sharing your successes with friends and loved ones, or simply taking a moment to reflect on how far

you've come, acknowledging your achievements
will help keep you motivated and inspired to
keep moving forward.

7. **Stay committed:** Finally, remember that making
plans is just the first step—staying committed to
following through on them is equally important.
Hold yourself accountable for taking action
toward your goals and stay focused on the
positive changes you're making in your life.

By incorporating these strategies into your planning
process, you can harness the power of proactive goal-setting
and create a roadmap for navigating the challenges of heartbreak with confidence, resilience, and determination.
Remember, dear friends, that you are the author of your
own story, and with a little planning and perseverance, you
can create a future that is bright, hopeful, and filled with
endless possibilities.

Making Things Happen

Now that we've delved into the art of making plans, let's talk
about the equally important task of turning those plans into
reality. After all, as comforting as it may be to have a
roadmap for the future, it's the steps we take to bring those
plans to life that truly make a difference in our healing
journey.

Plans are like seeds—they hold the potential for growth
and transformation, but it's only when we nurture them
with action that they can truly flourish. While it's essential
to set goals and make plans, it's equally crucial to take
consistent, intentional steps toward making those plans a
reality. Here's why:

- **Empowerment:** Taking action toward your goals empowers you to reclaim control over your life and shape your future in a way that aligns with your desires and values. By actively working toward the things that matter to you, you assert your agency and autonomy, fostering a sense of empowerment and self-efficacy in the process.
- **Progress:** Action is the catalyst for progress. While planning provides a roadmap for achieving your goals, it's the steps you take along the way that move you closer to success. By consistently taking action, you make steady progress toward your objectives, building momentum and confidence with each step forward.
- **Overcoming fear:** Taking action in the face of uncertainty or fear is a powerful act of courage and resilience. It requires you to confront your fears head-on, step outside of your comfort zone, and embrace the unknown with bravery and determination. By taking action despite your fears, you demonstrate resilience and strength, proving to yourself that you are capable of overcoming any obstacle that stands in your way.
- **Learning and growth:** Action is a teacher like no other. It provides invaluable opportunities for learning, growth, and self-discovery as you navigate the ups and downs of pursuing your goals. Whether you succeed or stumble along the way, each experience offers valuable lessons and insights that contribute to your personal and professional development.

- **Creating momentum:** Action begets action. As you take consistent steps toward your goals, you create momentum that propels you forward, making it easier to stay motivated and focused on your objectives. Momentum breeds success, and the more you take action, the more momentum you build, creating a positive feedback loop that fuels your progress.

Now that we understand the importance of taking action, let's explore some strategies for turning your plans into reality:

- **Set deadlines:** Deadlines create a sense of urgency and accountability, motivating you to take action and make progress toward your goals. Set realistic deadlines for each task or milestone along the way, and commit to meeting them to stay on track and maintain momentum.
- **Stay focused:** Distractions abound in our modern world, making it easy to lose focus and veer off course. Stay focused on your goals by minimizing distractions, setting boundaries, and creating a conducive environment for productivity. Prioritize your time and energy toward activities that align with your goals, and avoid getting sidetracked by less important tasks or distractions.
- **Seek support:** Don't be afraid to reach out for support when you need it. Whether it's seeking advice from a mentor, enlisting the help of friends and family, or joining a support group, surrounding yourself with a supportive network

of people who believe in you and your goals can provide invaluable encouragement, guidance, and accountability along the way.

- **Practice self-compassion:** Be gentle with yourself as you work toward your goals. Remember that healing and progress are not linear, and it's okay to experience setbacks or moments of self-doubt along the way. Practice self-compassion by treating yourself with kindness, understanding, and acceptance, especially during challenging times. Offer yourself the same level of care and compassion that you would offer to a dear friend facing similar struggles, and remember that you are worthy of love, kindness, and support every step of the way.

- **Visualize success:** Take time each day to visualize yourself achieving your goals and living the life you desire. Close your eyes and imagine yourself taking confident, decisive action toward your objectives, overcoming obstacles with grace and resilience, and ultimately reaching the finish line with a sense of accomplishment and fulfillment. Visualizing success can help you stay motivated, focused, and committed to your goals, even when faced with adversity or doubt. By cultivating a clear mental image of your desired outcome, you can harness the power of visualization to fuel your determination and drive as you work toward making your dreams a reality.

Creating Your Very Own Bucket List

Let's dive into creating your very own bucket list and filling it with exciting and meaningful experiences:

How to Make a Bucket List

Creating a bucket list is an exhilarating way to set goals, dream big, and make the most out of life. Here's how you can get started:

1. Take some time to reflect on the things that bring you joy, excitement, and fulfillment. Consider your hobbies, interests, and aspirations, both big and small.
2. Identify specific goals and experiences that you want to accomplish or try in your lifetime. These can range from adventurous activities to personal achievements to meaningful moments with loved ones.
3. Think about what matters most to you and align your bucket list items with your values and priorities. Choose experiences that resonate with your beliefs and bring you closer to living a life that feels authentic and fulfilling.
4. While it's important to dream big, it's also essential to be realistic about what you can achieve and when. Set achievable goals that challenge you to step out of your comfort zone and grow, but also allow yourself to dream beyond your current limitations.
5. Include a variety of experiences on your bucket list, ranging from small, everyday joys to grand

adventures. Mix in activities that you can do
alone, with friends or family, and those that push
your boundaries in new and exciting ways.

6. Your bucket list is not set in stone. It's okay to
add, remove, or modify items as your interests
and priorities evolve over time. Let your bucket
list grow and change with you as you continue to
explore life's possibilities.

Tips for Creating Your Bucket List

Here are some additional tips to help you create a
bucket list that inspires and motivates you:

- Instead of vague goals like "travel more," be
  specific about the destinations you want to visit
  or the experiences you want to have in each
  place.
- Focus on experiences rather than material
  possessions. Think about the memories you want
  to create and the adventures you want to
  embark on.
- Break larger goals into smaller, actionable steps
  to make them more manageable and achievable.
  This will help you stay motivated and track your
  progress along the way.
- Don't be afraid to include goals that push you out
  of your comfort zone and challenge you to grow.
  Embrace the opportunity to learn new skills,
  overcome fears, and expand your horizons.
- Celebrate your accomplishments and milestones
  as you check items off your bucket list. Take time

to savor the moment and reflect on how far
you've come.

Now, let's explore some fun and unique bucket list ideas
to inspire you on your journey.

Bucket List Ideas

1. Skydiving or bungee jumping
2. Learning to surf or snowboard
3. Taking a spontaneous road trip
4. Volunteering abroad
5. Swimming with dolphins or sharks
6. Learning a new language
7. Camping under the stars
8. Attending a music festival
9. Going on a hot air balloon ride
10. Visiting all seven continents
11. Participating in a marathon or triathlon
12. Taking a cooking or art class
13. Writing a book or starting a blog
14. Going on a safari in Africa
15. Learning to play a musical instrument
16. Watching the sunrise from a mountaintop
17. Going on a meditation retreat
18. Scuba diving in the Great Barrier Reef
19. Riding in a helicopter
20. Going on a cross-country road trip
21. Visiting ancient ruins or historical landmarks
22. Learning to dance salsa or tango
23. Completing a challenging hike or climb
24. Going on a wildlife photography expedition
25. Trying a new cuisine from around the world
26. Swimming in a bioluminescent bay

27. Going on a sailing adventure
28. Attending a traditional cultural festival
29. Starting a garden or growing your own food
30. Going on a backpacking trip through Europe

As we wrap up our exploration of channeling heartbreak energy into productive pursuits, get ready for the next step in your journey. Transitioning from purposeful engagement, we shift our focus to the empowering journey of self-compassion. In the following chapter, we'll uncover the keys to personal growth and resilience amidst heartbreak. Prepare to navigate the path with grace and self-love as you discover your true identity. Stay tuned for an insightful exploration of self-compassion and resilience, empowering you to emerge stronger from the challenges of heartbreak.

4

L—LIBERATE YOUR INNER SELF

In the end you don't so much find yourself as you find someone who knows who you are.

— ROBERT BRAULT

Chapter 4 is all about uncovering the essence of who you are—the strength, resilience, and authenticity that resides within. It's about embarking on a journey of self-discovery and self-compassion as you navigate through the tumultuous waters of heartbreak. By embracing your inner self, you pave the way for personal growth, empowerment, and transformation. So, buckle up and get ready to embark on a journey of liberation and self-realization. Together, we'll explore the depths of your inner being and emerge stronger and more resilient than ever before.

Why the Most Important Journey is the Journey Within

You see, amidst the chaos of heartbreak, there's a profound opportunity for self-discovery—a chance to unearth the treasures hidden within the depths of your being.

Let's talk about why this journey is absolutely crucial.

When we experience heartbreak, it's not just the external loss of a relationship that shakes us to our core. It's the internal rupture—the shattering of our sense of self, identity, and worth—that truly rocks our world. It's as if the person we loved was a mirror reflecting back to us our own beauty, value, and significance. And when that mirror shatters, it's not just the reflection that breaks apart; it's our sense of self that splinters into countless fragments.

In the aftermath of heartbreak, we find ourselves sifting through the wreckage, desperately searching for those missing pieces of ourselves. We feel lost, incomplete, and vulnerable, as if a vital part of us has been ripped away. It's a deeply disorienting and painful experience, leaving us grappling with questions of who we are, what we're worth, and whether we'll ever feel whole again.

But here's the glimmer of hope in the darkness: those missing pieces aren't lost forever. They're not scattered irretrievably into the abyss. Instead, they're waiting patiently within the depths of our being, ready to be reclaimed and reintegrated into the tapestry of our lives.

You see, the beauty of the human spirit lies in its resilience—the ability to heal, grow, and transform even in the face of the most devastating losses. Just as a broken bone knits itself back together, so too can our shattered sense of self mend and rebuild itself. It's a process of gathering up the fragments, examining them with compassion and curiosity, and piecing them back together with love and intention.

And as we embark on this journey of self-discovery, we come to realize that the person we were before heartbreak is not the same as the person we are destined to become. We have the power to redefine ourselves, to rewrite our stories, and to emerge from the ashes of our pain stronger, wiser, and more resilient than ever before.

So, if you're feeling lost amidst the ruins of heartbreak, remember this: you are not broken beyond repair. You are a mosaic of experiences, emotions, and dreams waiting to be rediscovered and reassembled. The journey to wholeness begins within you, and the missing pieces of yourself are waiting patiently to be found.

Now, let's talk about how self-discovery can help you heal from heartbreak.

When you take the time to explore your inner landscape, you gain a deeper understanding of your needs, desires, and boundaries. You learn to differentiate between what truly fulfills you and what merely distracts you from your pain. This self-awareness acts as a compass, guiding you toward decisions and actions that align with your authentic self.

Moreover, self-discovery is an act of self-love. By delving into the depths of your being, you're sending a powerful message to yourself—that you are worthy of exploration, growth, and transformation. And let me tell you, there's nothing more healing than showering yourself with unconditional love and acceptance, especially in the aftermath of heartbreak.

But self-discovery isn't just about finding yourself; it's about creating yourself. It's about embracing the power to redefine who you are and who you want to become. In the wake of heartbreak, you have a blank canvas before you—a chance to paint your life with bold strokes of authenticity and purpose.

So, my dear friend, if you're ready to embark on the most important journey of your life, buckle up and get ready to explore the depths of your soul. Together, we'll navigate the twists and turns, the highs and lows, and emerge stronger, wiser, and more radiant than ever before.

How to Find Yourself

Self-discovery is like setting sail on a voyage to uncover the treasures hidden within the depths of your being. It's about peeling back the layers, exploring the nooks and crannies of your soul, and embracing the full spectrum of who you are —especially in the wake of heartbreak, when pieces of yourself may feel lost or shattered.

So, if you're ready to embark on this transformative quest of self-discovery, let's dive in together. Here are some empowering tips, techniques, and exercises to help you kickstart your journey:

- **Start a morning journaling practice:** Begin your day with a ritual of self-reflection by adopting a morning journaling practice. Set aside time each morning to engage in stream-of-consciousness writing, also known as "morning pages." Allow your thoughts to flow freely onto the pages without judgment or expectation. Use this sacred space to express your desires, fears, and aspirations, and to gain insights into your inner world. For example, you might jot down your thoughts on what brings you joy, what challenges you're facing, and what dreams you're nurturing. By engaging in this daily practice, you'll cultivate self-awareness and deepen your connection with your innermost thoughts and feelings.

- **Take an audit of your relationships:** Conduct a brave and honest inventory of your relationships to determine where you may need to set boundaries and prioritize your well-being. Reflect on the dynamics of your relationships and identify any patterns of behavior that leave you feeling drained or unfulfilled. Consider asking yourself questions like: Where do I feel resentful or unseen in my relationships? Are there individuals who consistently violate my boundaries or take advantage of my kindness? By gaining clarity on your relational boundaries, you'll empower yourself to cultivate healthier connections and protect your emotional energy.

- **Make a list of things that delight you:** Take a moment to identify the simple pleasures and experiences that bring you joy and fulfillment. Create two lists: One of things that enhance your sense of ease and delight, and another of things that hinder it. For instance, you might discover that spending time in nature, practicing creative activities, or connecting with loved ones brings you immense joy. Conversely, certain stressors or obligations may detract from your well-being. By discerning what brings you joy and what drains your energy, you can make conscious choices to

prioritize activities and relationships that
nourish your soul.

- **Lean into a daily spiritual practice:** Cultivate a
daily spiritual practice, such as meditation or
yoga, to nurture your inner landscape and
cultivate a sense of peace and presence. Set aside
time each day to quiet your mind, connect with
your breath, and tune into the wisdom of your
inner being. Whether you prefer guided
meditation sessions, mindful movement
practices, or silent contemplation, find a spiritual
practice that resonates with your soul. By
incorporating spirituality into your daily routine,
you'll deepen your connection with yourself and
cultivate inner resilience in the face of life's
challenges.

- **Have a thoughtful, loving conversation with
your inner child:** Revisit the inner child within
you and engage in a compassionate dialogue
with this tender aspect of yourself. Reflect on
your childhood experiences, wishes, and
wounds, and offer your inner child the love,
validation, and comfort they may have yearned
for. Imagine sitting down with your younger self
and offering words of encouragement,
reassurance, and support. Acknowledge the pain
and struggles they endured, and affirm their
inherent worthiness and resilience. By nurturing
your inner child, you'll heal past wounds and
embrace a newfound sense of wholeness and
self-compassion.

- **Consider leaving your comfort zone:** Embrace
the discomfort of growth by stepping outside

your comfort zone and embracing new opportunities for exploration and expansion. Challenge yourself to take calculated risks, pursue bold aspirations, and venture into uncharted territory. Whether it's embarking on a solo adventure, starting a passion project, or initiating a difficult conversation, dare to push past the limits of familiarity and embrace the exhilaration of growth. Remember that true self-discovery often occurs when we dare to embrace the unknown and embrace the full spectrum of our potential.

Remember that the journey of self-discovery is a deeply personal and transformative odyssey. It's a sacred quest of unraveling the layers of your being, embracing your authentic self, and embracing the fullness of who you are.

Figuring Out Your Triggers

Emotional triggers are the hidden landmines of our psyche, waiting to detonate at the slightest provocation, sending us spiraling back into the depths of our pain. But fear not, for armed with self-awareness and resilience, you can navigate these triggers with grace and poise.

Firstly, let's identify what exactly an emotional trigger is. Picture this: you're scrolling through social media, and suddenly, you stumble upon a photo of your ex smiling with someone new. Instantly, a surge of sadness washes over you, and before you know it, you're plunged into a whirlpool of emotions—anger, jealousy, longing—all triggered by that seemingly innocuous image.

Now, recognizing your emotional triggers is key to

disarming their power over you. Take a moment to reflect on past experiences of heartbreak. What situations, memories, or stimuli tend to evoke strong emotional responses in you? It could be anything from hearing a particular song that reminds you of your ex to visiting a place where you shared special moments together.

Let's say, for example, that seeing happy couples in public triggers feelings of loneliness and despair in you. Instead of avoiding such situations altogether (which is neither feasible nor healthy), consider reframing your perspective. Remind yourself that your worth and happiness are not dependent on your relationship status. Practice self-compassion and focus on nurturing your own well-being, regardless of external circumstances.

Now, once you've identified your triggers, it's time to develop strategies for managing them effectively. Let's continue with our example of feeling triggered by seeing happy couples. One approach could be to cultivate a sense of gratitude for the love and companionship you've experienced in the past, rather than dwelling on feelings of lack or inadequacy.

Another strategy is to engage in activities that bring you joy and fulfillment, whether it's pursuing a hobby, spending time with friends, or volunteering for a cause you're passionate about. By filling your life with positivity and purpose, you create a buffer against the sting of emotional triggers.

Moreover, practicing mindfulness can help you stay grounded in the present moment rather than getting swept away by intrusive thoughts and emotions. When you notice yourself starting to feel triggered, take a deep breath and bring your attention back to the sensations in your body.

Remind yourself that you are safe and supported, and that these feelings will pass in time.

Lastly, don't hesitate to seek support from trusted friends, family members, or a professional therapist. Talking openly about your triggers and emotions can provide invaluable insight and validation, helping you feel less alone in your healing journey.

In summary, recognizing and managing your emotional triggers is an essential step in the process of healing from heartbreak. By cultivating self-awareness, practicing self-compassion, and seeking support when needed, you can navigate these triggers with resilience and grace, emerging stronger and more empowered on the other side. Remember, you are capable of overcoming any obstacle that stands in your way, and your journey to healing begins with honoring and embracing your inner strength.

Determining Where You Draw the Line

Boundaries are the invisible lines that define our sense of self-respect, autonomy, and emotional well-being. Boundaries are like the fences around our emotional garden, protecting us from trespassers who might trample our flowers or disrupt our peace.

Firstly, let's highlight the importance of boundaries in the context of healing from heartbreak. When we experience the pain of a breakup or betrayal, it's easy to lose sight of where we end and others begin. We might find ourselves bending over backward to accommodate our ex's needs or sacrificing our own happiness for the sake of salvaging a relationship. But here's the truth: Without healthy boundaries, we leave ourselves vulnerable to further hurt and exploitation.

So, what exactly distinguishes healthy boundaries from unhealthy ones? Healthy boundaries are like sturdy walls that safeguard our emotional well-being without shutting others out completely. They allow us to assert our needs, preferences, and limits in a respectful yet assertive manner. Unhealthy boundaries, on the other hand, are either too porous (allowing others to overstep our boundaries with impunity) or too rigid (isolating us from meaningful connections and experiences).

Now, how do you know if you need to shore up your boundaries? Here are a few telltale signs:

1. You feel resentful or drained after interacting with certain people.
2. You struggle to say no or assert your needs in relationships.
3. You find yourself constantly sacrificing your own well-being to please others.
4. You feel guilty or anxious about setting boundaries for fear of upsetting or disappointing others.

If any of these sound familiar, it might be time to reassess and strengthen your boundaries.

Setting and protecting your boundaries is a skill that requires practice and self-awareness. Here's how you can get started:

- **Identify your values and priorities:** Take some time to reflect on what matters most to you in life —whether it's honesty, respect, or personal integrity. These values will serve as the guiding principles for setting your boundaries.

- **Communicate assertively:** When asserting your boundaries, it's essential to communicate clearly, directly, and respectfully. Use "I" statements to express your needs and preferences without blaming or accusing others. For example, instead of saying, "You always make me feel ignored," try saying, "I feel hurt when my opinions are dismissed."

- **Practice self-care:** Prioritize self-care practices that nourish your body, mind, and spirit. Whether it's setting aside time for relaxation, engaging in hobbies that bring you joy, or seeking support from loved ones, self-care is essential for maintaining healthy boundaries.

- **Learn to say no:** Saying no is a powerful act of self-preservation. Practice saying no to requests or obligations that don't align with your values or priorities, even if it feels uncomfortable at first. Remember, saying no to others is saying yes to yourself.

- **Establish consequences:** It's essential to establish consequences for boundary violations and follow through with them. Whether it's ending a toxic relationship, stepping back from a draining situation, or asserting yourself in the face of disrespect, setting consequences reinforces the importance of your boundaries.

- **Seek support:** Don't hesitate to seek support from friends, family members, or a therapist as you navigate the process of setting and protecting your boundaries. Surround yourself with people who respect and support your journey toward healing and self-discovery.

In conclusion, setting and protecting your boundaries is a vital aspect of healing from heartbreak and reclaiming your sense of self-worth and empowerment. By identifying your values, communicating assertively, practicing self-care, learning to say no, establishing consequences, and seeking support, you can create healthy boundaries that honor your needs and foster healthy, fulfilling relationships. Remember you deserve to feel safe, respected, and valued in all your interactions, and boundaries are the key to making that a reality.

Identifying Your Why

Let's set off on a journey of self-discovery to uncover your "why"—the driving force behind your existence and the source of inspiration that propels you forward, especially in the aftermath of heartbreak. Your "why" is like the North Star guiding your life's journey, illuminating your path with purpose and meaning.

Now, how do you go about identifying your "why"? It's not always a straightforward process, but asking yourself probing questions can help unearth the underlying motivations and passions that fuel your soul. Here are some unique questions to consider:

What makes you come alive?: Think back to moments in your life when you felt most energized, engaged, and fulfilled. What were you doing? What activities or pursuits sparked a sense of joy and enthusiasm within you? Whether it's painting, volunteering, or exploring nature, pay attention to the activities that light up your spirit.

What are you naturally good at?: Reflect on your innate talents, skills, and strengths. What comes effortlessly to you? What activities do you excel in without much effort? Your natural abilities often provide clues about your purpose and calling in life. For example, if you have a knack for listening and offering support to others, you might find fulfillment in roles that involve mentoring or counseling.

What challenges have you overcome?: Consider the obstacles, setbacks, and hardships you've faced in life. How have these experiences shaped you? What lessons have you learned along the way? Sometimes, our greatest challenges provide the catalyst for discovering our purpose and resilience. For instance, if you've navigated through a difficult breakup, you may feel drawn to helping others heal from similar experiences.

What impact do you want to make?: Envision the legacy you wish to leave behind and the impact you aspire to have on the world. How do you want to contribute to the lives of others? What positive change do you hope to effect? Your desire to make a difference can serve as a powerful compass guiding your actions and decisions.

What brings you a sense of fulfillment?: Reflect on the activities, experiences, or relationships that bring you deep satisfaction and fulfillment. What moments leave you feeling content, gratified, and at peace with yourself? Whether it's connecting with loved ones, pursuing creative endeavors, or making meaningful contributions to your community, identify the sources of fulfillment that resonate with your heart.

What values do you hold dear?: Consider the core values that define who you are and what you stand for. What principles guide your actions and decisions? Your values serve as the moral compass guiding your life's direction and influencing your choices. For example, if integrity, compassion, and justice are important to you, you may feel called to advocate for social causes or pursue a career in service-oriented fields.

What excites and energizes you?: Pay attention to the topics, ideas, or activities that ignite your curiosity and passion. What subjects do you find yourself researching or discussing with enthusiasm? What dreams or aspirations spark a fire within you? Your passions and interests can provide valuable clues about your purpose and direction in life.

As you explore these questions and delve into the depths of your heart and soul, remember that your "why" may evolve and change over time. It's a journey of self-discovery that requires patience, introspection, and self-compassion. Embrace the process with an open mind and heart, trusting that you hold the answers within you.

In conclusion, identifying your "why" is a transformative journey that can illuminate your path with purpose, meaning, and fulfillment. By asking yourself probing questions, reflecting on your passions, talents, challenges, and values, you can uncover the underlying motivations that drive you forward and inspire you to live a life aligned with your true essence. Remember, your "why" is the guiding star that leads you toward a life of authenticity, joy, and contribution to the world.

Journal Prompts to Get to Know Yourself a Little Better

Let's dive into some thought-provoking journal prompts to help you deepen your self-discovery journey and foster greater self-awareness:

1. What are my core values, and how do they shape my decisions and actions?

2. What are my greatest strengths, and how can I leverage them to achieve my goals?

3. What are some limiting beliefs or self-doubts that hold me back, and how can I challenge them?

4. Reflect on a challenging experience from your past. What lessons did you learn from it?

5. Describe a moment when you felt truly alive and fulfilled. What were the circumstances, and what made it meaningful?

6. What activities or hobbies bring me a sense of joy and fulfillment? How can I incorporate more of them into my life?

7. Think about the people you admire. What qualities do they possess that you admire, and how can you cultivate those qualities within yourself?

8. Consider a time when you faced adversity or failure. How did you overcome it, and what strengths did you discover in the process?

9. Reflect on your relationships with others. What patterns or dynamics do you notice, and how do they reflect your inner world?

10. What are some dreams or aspirations that you've been hesitant to pursue? What steps can you take to move closer to them?

11. Describe your ideal day from start to finish. What activities would you engage in, and how would you feel throughout the day?

12. Reflect on your relationship with self-care and self-love. In what ways do you prioritize your well-being, and how can you nurture yourself more deeply?

13. Consider a role model or mentor who has had a significant impact on your life. What lessons have you learned from them, and how do they inspire you?

14. What are some fears or insecurities that hold you back from fully expressing yourself? How can you cultivate courage and authenticity in spite of them?

15. Reflect on a recent moment of gratitude or appreciation. What or who are you thankful for, and why?

16. Consider your ideal future self. What qualities or achievements do you envision, and what steps can you take to align with that vision?

17. Think about a time when you felt deeply connected to nature or the world around you. What insights or feelings did you experience in that moment?

18. Reflect on your relationship with time and productivity. How do you currently manage your time, and what changes would you like to make?

19. Consider a recent setback or disappointment. How can you reframe it as an opportunity for growth and resilience?

20. Reflect on your childhood dreams and aspirations. How have they evolved over time, and which ones still hold meaning for you?

21. What are some self-care practices that nourish your mind, body, and spirit? How can you integrate them into your daily routine?

22. Consider the people you surround yourself with. Do they uplift and support you, or do they drain

your energy? How can you cultivate healthier relationships?

23. Reflect on a recent challenge or obstacle you faced. What strengths or resources did you draw upon to overcome it?

24. Think about a time when you felt completely in flow or aligned with your purpose. What were you doing, and how can you recreate that feeling more often?

25. Consider your relationship with failure. How do you typically respond to setbacks, and how can you adopt a more resilient mindset?

26. Reflect on your ideal career or vocation. What skills, passions, and values do you want to align with in your professional life?

27. Consider a recent act of kindness or generosity. How did it impact you and others, and how can you cultivate more compassion in your life?

28. Reflect on your relationship with creativity. What forms of self-expression bring you joy, and how can you nurture your creative spirit?

29. Think about a time when you felt truly connected to yourself and others. What factors contributed to that sense of connection, and how can you cultivate it more intentionally?

30. Consider your relationship with success and achievement. How do you define success, and what goals or milestones are important to you?

As we wrap up our journey of liberating your inner self, the path ahead shines with the promise of reclaiming your identity. Through self-compassion, you've unearthed reservoirs of strength and resilience within. In our next chapter, we embark on a profound exploration of healing and self-love. Together, we'll navigate the complexities of letting go, infusing your journey with the nurturing embrace of self-compassion. With each step, you'll find yourself closer to regaining control and embracing the newfound freedom that comes with honoring your true self.

5

A—ASSEMBLE YOUR HEART

If you have the ability to love, love yourself first.

— CHARLES BUKOWSKI

In this chapter, we delve into the intricate process of rebuilding your sense of self and regaining control over your life after the tumult of heartbreak. It's about piecing together the fragments of your heart with tenderness and self-compassion, acknowledging that while the journey may be challenging, it is also profoundly empowering. By confronting the end of your relationship and embracing the profound significance of self-love, you embark on a journey of self-discovery and renewal. Together, we'll navigate the complexities of letting go, forging a path toward wholeness and fulfillment. So, let's start this transformative journey of self-assembly, where every step brings you closer to reclaiming your identity and embracing the boundless love that resides within you.

Accepting the End For a New Beginning

Accepting the end of a relationship is tough. It's like trying to swallow a bitter pill that just won't go down. But here's the thing: until you swallow that bitter truth, you can't begin to rebuild. Think of it like renovating a house —you can't start remodeling until you acknowledge that the old structure has served its purpose and needs to come down.

So why is accepting the end so crucial? Well, let me break it down for you.

First off, denial only prolongs the pain. Holding onto hope that things will magically work out keeps you stuck in a perpetual state of limbo. You're neither here nor there, unable to move forward. It's like being stuck in quicksand— the more you struggle, the deeper you sink.

Acceptance, on the other hand, is like grabbing hold of a sturdy branch to pull yourself out. It's the acknowledgment that the relationship has run its course and that it's time to release it with grace. Now, acceptance doesn't mean you have to be thrilled about it. It's okay to feel sad, angry, or even relieved. Emotions are messy, and that's perfectly normal.

But how do you come to terms with the end? Well, let's break it down into manageable steps.

Step 1: Feel your feelings. This might sound obvious, but it's essential. Allow yourself to grieve the loss of the relationship. Cry, scream, punch a pillow—do whatever you need to do to let those emotions out. Bottling them up only leads to more pain down the road.

Step 2: Reflect on the relationship. Take some time to think about what went wrong and what you learned from the experience. Every relationship, no matter how painful, teaches us valuable lessons about ourselves and what we want in a partner. Use this knowledge to grow and evolve.

Step 3: Practice self-compassion. Be gentle with yourself during this time of transition. It's okay to make mistakes, to feel lost, to not have all the answers. Treat yourself with the same kindness and understanding that you would offer a close friend going through a tough time.

Step 4: Focus on the present moment. It's easy to get caught up in "what ifs" and "could have beens," but dwelling on the past only keeps you stuck. Instead, try to stay grounded in the present. Take up mindfulness practices like meditation or yoga to help you stay centered and focused.

Step 5: Look to the future with hope. While it's important to acknowledge the pain of the past, it's equally important to look forward with optimism. Remember that the end of one chapter is the beginning of another. You have the power to create a bright and fulfilling future for yourself, one that is not defined by your past relationships.

Finding Yourself Again

Alright, let's tackle the big one: finding yourself again after heartbreak. It's like trying to navigate through a dense fog— you know where you want to go, but you can't see the path ahead clearly. But fear not, my friend, because clarity is just around the corner.

First things first, let's talk about how heartbreak can mess with your confidence and self-image. Picture this: you were cruising along, feeling pretty good about yourself and your life, and then BAM! The rug gets pulled out from under you, and suddenly you're questioning everything. Your once-rock-solid confidence takes a hit, and you start to doubt your worth and value.

Signs you need a confidence boost? Oh, they're not hard to spot. Do you find yourself constantly comparing yourself to your ex's new partner? Do you shy away from social situations because you feel like you're not good enough? Or maybe you're overly critical of yourself, nitpicking every flaw and mistake. Yeah, those are all red flags that your confidence could use a little TLC.

But don't worry because rebuilding confidence and a positive self-image is totally doable. Here are a few strategies to get you started:

- Practice self-affirmations. I know, I know, it sounds cheesy, but trust me, it works. Start each day by looking in the mirror and saying something positive about yourself. It could be as simple as "I am strong" or "I am worthy of love." Repeat these affirmations throughout the day whenever you start to doubt yourself.
- Celebrate your strengths. Take some time to make a list of all the things you're good at. Maybe you're a great listener, or maybe you have a killer sense of humor. Whatever it is, own it! Remind yourself of your strengths whenever you start to feel insecure.
- Set achievable goals. Break down your bigger goals into smaller, more manageable tasks. Each time you accomplish one of these tasks, you'll get a little boost of confidence. Plus, achieving your goals will give you a sense of purpose and direction.
- Surround yourself with positive influences. Spend time with friends and family who lift you up and make you feel good about yourself. Avoid

toxic people who bring you down or make you question your worth.

- Take care of yourself. This means prioritizing self-care activities like exercise, healthy eating, and getting enough sleep. When you take care of your body and mind, you'll feel better about yourself overall.

Remember, rebuilding confidence is a process, not an overnight transformation. Be patient with yourself and celebrate every small victory along the way. You've got this!

Letting Go of Guilt and Shame

Guilt and shame are two emotions that can weigh us down like a ton of bricks, especially after experiencing heartbreak. But guess what? It's time to kick them to the curb and reclaim your peace of mind.

First, let's define what we're dealing with here. Toxic guilt and shame are like the evil twins of self-blame. Guilt is that nagging feeling that you've done something wrong or caused harm to someone else, while shame is the belief that you are inherently flawed or unworthy of love and acceptance.

Now, here's the thing about guilt and shame—they're not just uninvited guests at the pity party; they're downright dangerous. When left unchecked, they can wreak havoc on our mental and emotional well-being, keeping us stuck in a cycle of self-loathing and despair.

So, how do we break free from the clutches of guilt and shame? Here are a few strategies to help you ditch the baggage and move forward with grace:

- **Self-compassion is your golden ticket to freedom.** Treat yourself with the same kindness and understanding that you would offer to a dear friend in need. Remind yourself that you are human, and humans make mistakes. It's all part of the journey.
- **Challenge negative thoughts.** When guilt and shame rear their ugly heads, don't just accept them as gospel truth. Challenge them! Ask yourself, "Is this thought really serving me? Is it based on fact, or is it just a product of my inner critic run amok?" More often than not, you'll find that these thoughts are nothing more than hot air.
- **Practice forgiveness.** And no, I'm not just talking about forgiving others—I'm talking about forgiving yourself. Let go of any resentment or anger you're holding onto toward yourself for past mistakes or perceived shortcomings. Remember, forgiveness is not about condoning or excusing behavior; it's about setting yourself free from the burden of carrying around all that emotional baggage.
- **Focus on self-improvement.** Instead of wallowing in guilt and shame, channel that energy into something positive. Set goals for personal growth and development, and take concrete steps toward achieving them. Whether it's learning a new skill, volunteering in your community, or embarking on a journey of self-discovery, find ways to invest in yourself and your future.

- **Seek support.** You don't have to go it alone, my friend. Reach out to friends, family, or a therapist for support and guidance. Talking about your feelings with someone you trust can help you gain perspective and let go of the shame and guilt that's been weighing you down.
- **Practice mindfulness.** Bring your awareness to the present moment and let go of the past. Engage in activities like meditation, deep breathing, or yoga to quiet your mind and cultivate inner peace. Remember, you have the power to choose where you focus your attention —choose wisely.
- **Release the need for perfection.** News flash: nobody's perfect! Let go of the unrealistic expectations you've placed on yourself and embrace your imperfections. Remember, it's okay to stumble and fall along the way. The important thing is that you keep moving forward with courage and resilience.

In the end, letting go of guilt and shame is a journey— one that requires patience, self-compassion, and a whole lot of courage. But it's a journey worth taking.

Being Kind to Yourself

It's time to talk about one of the most important relation- ships you'll ever have—the one with yourself. Let's dial down the self-criticism and ramp up the self-compassion. Because guess what? You deserve it.

- **Practice self-love as a daily habit:** Think of self-love as a journey rather than a destination. It's not about achieving perfection or being in a constant state of adoration for yourself. Instead, it's about showing up for yourself every day, even when things get tough. Define what self-love means to you, whether it's acceptance, neutrality, or kindness, and make it a practice.

- **Separate your reality from self-worth:** Your worthiness isn't tied to your circumstances or achievements. Just like you love your friends and family despite their flaws, you can love yourself despite your imperfections. Embrace the concept of radical acceptance—acknowledge your reality without judgment, and focus on what you can control rather than dwelling on what you can't.

- **Challenge negative self-talk with facts:** When negative thoughts start creeping in, challenge them with evidence to the contrary. Look for objective truths that counteract your inner critic's narrative. By sticking to the facts, you can avoid spiraling into self-blame and instead cultivate a more balanced perspective.

- **Address intergenerational patterns:** Recognize and break free from negative patterns inherited from your upbringing. Whether it's hyper-critical parents or societal messages undermining your self-worth, challenge these narratives and forge a new path toward self-love.

- **Acknowledge the impact of trauma and oppression:** If you've experienced trauma or belong to marginalized groups, recognize the added challenges to self-love. Seek support from

a therapist to unpack these issues and prioritize
self-care practices that honor your body and
boundaries.

- **Set boundaries to protect your self-worth:**
Surround yourself with people who uplift and
respect you, and don't be afraid to distance
yourself from those who undermine your self-
esteem. Practice saying no to demands that drain
your energy and prioritize relationships built on
mutual respect and communication.
- **Remember, self-love is a worthwhile pursuit:**
Despite what social media may portray, self-love
isn't selfish or superficial. It's the foundation for
healthy relationships, personal growth, and
making a positive impact in the world. So,
embrace the journey of loving yourself, flaws and
all, and watch as it transforms every aspect of
your life.

By incorporating these practices into your daily life, you
can cultivate a deeper sense of self-compassion and
resilience, paving the way for healing and growth after
heartbreak. Remember, you are worthy of love, starting with
the love you give yourself. So, go ahead and be kind—to
yourself.

Find Your Support System

Finding your support system is one of the vital components
of your healing journey. Believe me, it's not just helpful; it's
absolutely essential, and I'm here to walk you through why
it holds such significance and how you can cultivate a
resilient one.

Why Do You Need a Support System?

First things first, let's talk about why having a support system is absolutely essential when you're navigating the stormy seas of heartbreak.

- **Emotional validation:** When you're going through heartbreak, it's easy to feel like you're drowning in a sea of emotions. Having a support system means having people who can validate your feelings, listen to you without judgment, and provide that much-needed shoulder to cry on.
- **Perspective and advice:** Sometimes, we get so caught up in our own thoughts and feelings that we can't see the bigger picture. Your support system can offer fresh perspectives and valuable advice, helping you gain clarity and make informed decisions.
- **Physical and practical support:** From helping you move out of your shared apartment to bringing over a tub of your favorite ice cream, your support system can provide practical assistance that eases the burden of heartbreak.
- **Combating isolation:** Heartbreak can be an incredibly isolating experience. Having a support system ensures that you're not going through it alone, reminding you that there are people who care about you and are there for you, no matter what.

How to Build a Solid Support System?

Now that you understand why a support system is

crucial, let's talk about how to build one that's strong and reliable.

- **Identify your existing support network:** Take a moment to think about the people in your life who you trust and feel comfortable opening up to. This could include friends, family members, colleagues, or even online communities.
- **Communicate your needs:** Once you've identified potential members of your support system, it's important to communicate your needs to them. Let them know what you're going through and how they can best support you during this time.
- **Diversify your support network:** While it's great to have a few close confidants, it's also helpful to diversify your support network. This means reaching out to different people for different types of support. For example, you might turn to a friend for emotional support, a family member for practical assistance, and a therapist for professional guidance.
- **Set boundaries:** While it's important to lean on your support system during tough times, it's also crucial to set boundaries to protect your own well-being. Make sure you're not overwhelming any one person with your needs and be respectful of their boundaries as well.
- **Be proactive in seeking support:** Don't wait for your support system to come to you—be proactive in reaching out for help when you need it. Whether it's scheduling regular check-ins with

a friend or booking therapy sessions, prioritize
your own healing and well-being.

- **Consider professional support if necessary:**
  While friends and family can offer invaluable
  support, sometimes you may need additional
  help from a professional. Don't hesitate to reach
  out to a therapist or counselor who specializes in
  helping people heal from heartbreak.

Remember, building a support system takes time and
effort, but it's one of the best investments you can make in
your own healing journey. Surround yourself with people
who uplift and support you, and don't be afraid to lean on
them when you need it most.

Being Ready to Love Again

Now, let's tackle the daunting but hopeful prospect of
opening your hearts once more after heartbreak. It may
seem like an impossible task right now, but trust me, it's
within your reach. Here are some gentle steps to guide you
through this process:

- **Allow yourself to heal:** Before diving into the
  idea of loving again, it's crucial to give yourself
  the time and space to heal from your previous
  relationship. Healing isn't a linear process, and
  it's okay to have good days and bad days. Give
  yourself permission to feel all the emotions that
  come your way without judgment or pressure.
  For example, if you find yourself feeling sad or
  angry about your past relationship, instead of
  pushing those emotions away, allow yourself to

sit with them. Journaling, talking to a trusted friend, or seeking therapy can be helpful ways to navigate these feelings.

- **Reflect on what you've learned:** Take some time to reflect on the lessons you've learned from your past relationship. What worked well? What didn't? Understanding these insights can help you approach future relationships with greater awareness and intention. For instance, you might realize that communication was a challenge in your previous relationship. As you prepare to love again, you can make a conscious effort to prioritize open and honest communication with future partners.

- **Rediscover yourself:** Use this time to reconnect with yourself and rediscover what brings you joy and fulfillment. Engage in activities and hobbies that nourish your soul and make you feel alive. Maybe you used to love painting but haven't picked up a brush in years. Or perhaps you've always wanted to try hiking but never had the chance. Reconnecting with these aspects of yourself can help you feel more grounded and confident as you prepare to open your heart again.

- **Set healthy boundaries:** As you navigate the journey of opening your heart to love again, it's essential to set healthy boundaries to protect yourself from potential hurt. Be clear about your needs and expectations in future relationships, and don't be afraid to communicate them openly. For example, you might decide that you need a partner who respects your need for alone time or someone who shares your values and life goals. Communicating these boundaries early on can help ensure that you're entering into relationships that align with your needs and desires.

- **Practice self-compassion:** Be gentle with yourself throughout this process. Healing from heartbreak and opening your heart to love again can be challenging, and it's okay to have moments of doubt or vulnerability. Practice self-compassion and remind yourself that you are worthy of love and happiness. If you find yourself struggling with self-doubt or self-criticism, try practicing self-affirmations or engaging in self-care activities that make you feel nurtured and supported.

- **Take things slowly:** Remember, there's no rush to jump into a new relationship. Take things at your own pace and honor your unique journey. Allow yourself to get to know potential partners gradually, and don't feel pressured to commit before you're ready. For instance, you might start by casually dating and getting to know different people without putting too much pressure on yourself to find "the one" right away. Taking things slowly can help you feel more comfortable and confident as you explore the possibility of love once again.

Remember, you deserve love, and when you're ready, it will be waiting for you with open arms.

Affirmations to Remind Yourself of How Great You Are

Here are 20 affirmations tailored to help you navigate the journey of healing from heartbreak:

1. I am resilient, and I can overcome any challenge that comes my way.
2. I am worthy of love and respect, regardless of my relationship status.
3. I trust in the timing of my life, knowing that everything happens for a reason.
4. I release the pain of my past and embrace the beauty of my present moment.
5. I am whole and complete, just as I am, and I don't need anyone else to validate my worth.
6. I forgive myself for any mistakes I've made and choose to learn and grow from them.
7. I am capable of healing from this heartbreak, and I will emerge stronger than ever before.
8. I allow myself to let go of what no longer serves me and make space for new blessings to enter my life.
9. I deserve happiness, and I am worthy of creating a life filled with love and joy.
10. I am not defined by my past experiences or failures; I am defined by my resilience and strength.
11. I trust in my ability to make healthy decisions for myself and create a future that aligns with my desires.
12. I am surrounded by love and support, even on the toughest days.

13. I honor my emotions and give myself permission to feel whatever comes up without judgment.

14. I release the need for closure and find peace in accepting things as they are.

15. I am grateful for the lessons I've learned from this experience and the growth it has inspired within me.

16. I choose to focus on the present moment and appreciate the beauty and blessings that surround me.

17. I am resilient like a phoenix rising from the ashes, and I will soar to new heights.

18. I am deserving of all the love and happiness the universe has to offer, and I welcome it into my life with open arms.

19. I trust in my inner wisdom to guide me toward the path of healing and self-discovery.

20. I am enough, exactly as I am, and I don't need anyone else's approval to validate my worth.

Remember, my dear friends, affirmations are not just words; they are powerful tools that can help rewire our brains and transform our beliefs about ourselves and the world around us.

Having tenderly guided yourself through reclaiming your identity and embracing self-love, you're now equipped with the tools to navigate the next phase of your healing journey. In the upcoming chapter, we delve into the transformative potential within adversity, inspiring you to emerge from the shadows of negative experiences not just healed but stronger, wiser, and more empowered than ever.

6

I—IGNITE YOUR POWER

We acquire the strength we have overcome.

— RALPH WALDO EMERSON

As we journey further along the path of healing, it's crucial to recognize the transformative potential that lies within our pain. While heartbreak may leave us feeling shattered and vulnerable, it also presents us with a unique opportunity for growth and empowerment.

In this chapter, we'll explore how adversity can serve as a catalyst for profound personal development. Instead of allowing our negative experiences to define us, we'll learn to harness the power within us to rise above them. Like a phoenix emerging from the ashes, we have the ability to transform our pain into strength and wisdom.

Throughout these pages, we'll discover how to cultivate resilience, tap into our inner resources, and embrace the challenges that come our way. By reframing our perspective and embracing the lessons that accompany hardship, we can emerge from our struggles stronger, wiser, and more empowered than ever before.

So, let's embark on this journey together, igniting the flames of our inner power and embracing the transformative potential of our experiences. Together, we'll discover the resilience and strength that resides within each of us, ready to guide us toward a brighter, more empowered future.

Building Resilience

In this section, we're delving into one of the most powerful tools in our emotional toolkit: resilience. It's that inner strength that helps us bounce back from adversity, navigate life's twists and turns, and emerge stronger than before.

Resilience isn't just about weathering the storm; it's about thriving in the midst of it. It's the ability to adapt to adversity, to bend without breaking, and to find meaning and growth in the face of challenges. Think of it as the sturdy foundation that keeps us standing tall even when life throws its toughest punches.

Now, you might be wondering: what exactly makes someone resilient? Well, it's a combination of factors, both internal and external. Internal factors include things like having a positive outlook, strong problem-solving skills, and the ability to regulate emotions. External factors, on the other hand, encompass things like supportive relationships, access to resources, and a sense of purpose or meaning in life.

Resilience isn't just a nice-to-have trait—it's an essential skill for navigating life's inevitable ups and downs. Here's why everyone needs resilience in their emotional toolkit:

- **Coping with adversity:** Life is full of challenges, from everyday stressors to major crises like loss, illness, or job loss. Resilience equips us with the tools to bounce back from these setbacks, to adapt to changing circumstances, and to persevere in the face of adversity.
- **Maintaining mental health:** Resilience is closely linked to mental well-being. It helps us cope with stress, manage negative emotions, and maintain a positive outlook even during difficult times. By building resilience, we can protect our mental health and reduce the risk of conditions like anxiety and depression.
- **Building stronger relationships:** Resilience isn't just about weathering personal storms—it's also about fostering strong, supportive relationships. When we're resilient, we're better able to communicate effectively, resolve conflicts, and offer support to those we care about. This, in turn, strengthens our social connections and enhances our overall well-being.
- **Achieving goals and dreams:** Resilience isn't just about surviving; it's about thriving. It's what enables us to set ambitious goals, overcome obstacles, and stay focused on our dreams even when the going gets tough. With resilience, we're better equipped to persevere in the pursuit of our passions and turn setbacks into opportunities for growth.
- **Thriving in uncertain times:** In today's fast-paced, ever-changing world, adaptability is key. Resilience helps us navigate uncertainty, embrace change, and thrive in the face of

constant flux. By cultivating resilience, we can
approach life's uncertainties with confidence and
resilience, knowing that we have the inner
strength to face whatever comes our way.

In short, resilience isn't just a nice bonus—it's a fundamental skill for living a fulfilling, meaningful life.

The 7 Cs of Resilience

Ah, the 7 Cs of resilience—a handy roadmap for navigating life's challenges with grace and strength. Let's break
them down:

1. **Calmness:** Ever notice how some people seem
   unflappable in the face of chaos? That's because
   they've mastered the art of staying calm under
   pressure. Whether it's through deep breathing,
   mindfulness, or simply taking a step back to
   regain perspective, finding your inner calm is key
   to building resilience.
2. **Confidence:** Believing in yourself is half the
   battle. When you have confidence in your
   abilities and trust in your capacity to overcome
   obstacles, you're already halfway to resilience.
   Remember, you've faced tough times before, and
   you've come out on top.
3. **Connection:** We're not meant to go it alone.
   Building strong, supportive relationships is
   essential for resilience. Surround yourself with
   people who lift you up, who believe in you, and
   who have your back no matter what. Together,
   you'll weather any storm.

4. **Character:** Your character—the sum total of your values, beliefs, and integrity—is the bedrock of resilience. It's what guides you through tough times, keeps you grounded in your principles, and helps you stay true to yourself no matter what life throws your way.

5. **Control:** While there's much in life that's beyond our control, there's also plenty that's within our grasp. Resilient individuals focus on what they can control—like their attitude, their actions, and their choices—rather than getting bogged down by things beyond their power.

6. **Commitment:** Resilience isn't just about bouncing back; it's about staying the course even when the going gets tough. It's about committing to your goals, your values, and your vision for the future, no matter how many obstacles stand in your way.

7. **Contribution:** Finally, resilience isn't just about helping yourself—it's also about helping others. When we contribute to something larger than ourselves—whether it's through acts of kindness, volunteering, or simply being there for someone in need—we not only strengthen our own resilience but also create a ripple effect of positivity in the world.

How to Be More Resilient

Now that we've covered the basics, let's talk about how you can cultivate resilience in your own life. Here are a few strategies to get you started:

- **Practice self-care:** Remember, you can't pour from an empty cup. Prioritize your physical, emotional, and mental well-being by making time for activities that nourish and replenish you.
- **Build a support network:** Surround yourself with people who lift you up and provide a shoulder to lean on when times get tough. Cultivate relationships built on trust, empathy, and mutual support.
- **Cultivate optimism:** Train your brain to focus on the positive by practicing gratitude, reframing negative thoughts, and seeking out silver linings even in the darkest of clouds.
- **Develop problem-solving skills:** Instead of getting overwhelmed by obstacles, break them down into manageable chunks and tackle them one step at a time. Look for creative solutions, seek advice from others, and don't be afraid to ask for help when you need it.
- **Find meaning in adversity:** Every setback is an opportunity for growth. Look for the lessons and the silver linings in difficult situations, and use them as fuel to propel you forward on your journey.
- **Embrace flexibility:** Life rarely goes according to plan, and that's okay! Learn to adapt to changing circumstances, pivot when necessary, and embrace the unexpected twists and turns along the way.
- **Practice self-compassion:** Be gentle with yourself, especially during tough times. Treat yourself with the same kindness, understanding,

and compassion that you would offer to a friend in need.

So there you have it—your crash course in resilience! Remember, building resilience is a journey, not a destination. It takes time, practice, and patience, but with perseverance and determination, you can cultivate the inner strength to weather any storm that comes your way.

Becoming a Stronger Person

Building mental toughness is like strengthening a muscle—it requires practice, dedication, and a willingness to push through discomfort. Here's how readers can develop the mental toughness needed to weather any obstacle that comes their way:

- **Use visualization:** Visualization is a powerful tool for managing stress and boosting confidence. Close your eyes and imagine a time when you successfully navigated a challenging situation. Recall the feelings of accomplishment and resilience that accompanied that experience. By visualizing past successes, you can cultivate the belief in your ability to overcome adversity.
- **Plan for setbacks:** Life is unpredictable, and setbacks are inevitable. Instead of dwelling on losses or misfortunes, focus on regaining your composure and moving forward. Having a plan in place for how to deal with setbacks can help you maintain perspective and resilience in the face of adversity.

- **Manage stress:** Stress is a natural part of life, but how we respond to it can make all the difference. Practice stress management techniques such as meditation, deep breathing, or progressive muscle relaxation to help you stay calm and focused during challenging times. Remember that you have control over your mental state and how you choose to respond to stressors.
- **Get more sleep:** Adequate sleep is essential for maintaining mental clarity and emotional resilience. Aim for seven to nine hours of sleep each night, or more if you're engaging in high-stress activities. Prioritize sleep as part of your self-care routine to ensure you're well-rested and ready to face whatever challenges come your way.
- **Avoid seeing crises as insurmountable problems:** It's easy to feel overwhelmed when faced with a crisis, but it's important to remember that challenges are temporary. Focus on the steps you can take to address the situation rather than fixating on the problem itself. Look for small victories and signs of progress to maintain a sense of hope and optimism.
- **Accept change as a part of living:** Change is inevitable, and learning to accept it can help build resilience. Embrace the idea that certain goals may no longer be attainable and focus on adapting to new circumstances. By accepting change, you free yourself from the burden of trying to control the uncontrollable.
- **Move toward your goals:** Break big goals down into smaller, manageable steps and take action

every day to move closer to achieving them. Celebrate small victories along the way, and remember that progress, no matter how small, is still progress. By taking decisive action toward your goals, you build confidence and resilience.

- **Look for opportunities for self-discovery:** Difficult situations can be opportunities for growth and self-discovery. Embrace challenges as learning experiences and focus on the lessons they can teach you. Use adversity as a chance to strengthen your relationships, increase your self-confidence, and deepen your sense of gratitude for life.

- **Nurture a positive view of yourself:** Confidence and self-belief are essential for building resilience. Cultivate a positive self-image by focusing on your strengths and accomplishments. Practice self-compassion and kindness toward yourself, especially during challenging times.

- **Keep things in perspective:** When faced with difficulties, maintain a long-term perspective and avoid blowing things out of proportion. Remember that setbacks are temporary and that you have the strength and resilience to overcome them. By keeping things in perspective, you can avoid becoming overwhelmed by challenges and maintain a sense of hope for the future.

- **Maintain a hopeful outlook:** Cultivate optimism and expect positive outcomes, even in the face of adversity. Visualize success and focus on the possibilities for growth and improvement. By maintaining a hopeful outlook, you can

approach challenges with confidence and
resilience, knowing that you have the inner
strength to overcome them.

In addition to these strategies, remember that cultivating
mental toughness is a personal journey, and what works for
one person may not work for another. Experiment with
different techniques such as journaling, practicing gratitude, or engaging in spiritual practices to find what
resonates with you. Ultimately, building mental toughness
takes time and effort, but the rewards—increased confidence, resilience, and emotional well-being—are well
worth it.

No Mistakes, Only Lessons Learned

Developing a growth mindset is all about turning those
stumbling blocks into stepping stones, transforming
setbacks into opportunities for growth and personal
improvement.

What Is Growth Mindset?

Simply put, growth mindset is the belief that your abilities and intelligence can be developed through dedication,
hard work, and learning from experiences. Instead of seeing
setbacks as permanent failures, those with a growth mindset
view them as temporary obstacles that can be overcome
with effort and perseverance.

Growth vs Fixed Mindset

Now, let's distinguish between a growth mindset and its
counterpart, the fixed mindset. A fixed mindset is character-
ized by the belief that your qualities and abilities are set in
stone, leading to a fear of failure and avoidance of challenges. On the other hand, a growth mindset embraces chal-

lenges, sees failures as opportunities to learn, and believes in the power of effort to improve skills and achieve success.

Tips on How to Cultivate a Growth Mindset

Shifting from a fixed mindset to a growth mindset isn't like flipping a light switch. It's a journey that requires conscious effort, practice, and self-reflection. But the good news? It's entirely possible, and I've got nine proven strategies to help you along the way.

Recognize Fixed Mindset Traps

The first step toward developing a growth mindset involves understanding its counterpart—the fixed mindset. These are ingrained beliefs that your abilities are static and unchangeable. Do you ever catch yourself coming across a weakness or flaw of yours and thinking, "Well, that's just the way I am," or crossing a roadblock and saying, "That's just how things are?" By flagging these, you can consciously choose to adopt a more adaptive mindset, viewing these situations as opportunities for learning and growth.

Embrace Challenges

An important step on your journey is to welcome challenges into your life. A person with a growth mindset views and responds to challenges by recognizing that they are not roadblocks on your path; they're opportunities to learn and grow. Change your perspective. See each challenge as a puzzle to solve, a mystery to unravel, or a game to win. It's about shifting from "I can't do this" to "I can't do this, yet." Remember, growth comes from stretching your abilities, stepping out of your comfort zone, and daring to do what you once thought impossible.

Don't Fear Failure

The next step? Redefine failure. People with a growth mindset don't see failure as a dead end. Instead, they view it as a learning experience—a stepping stone on their path to success. Failure isn't proof of incapacity; it's a testament to bravery for daring to try. So, the next time you fail, don't let it discourage you. Analyze what went wrong, learn from it, and use that knowledge to do better next time.

Value Effort

Recognize that effort is the engine that drives growth. Even when progress seems slow, your effort isn't wasted; it's building the resilience and strength you need to achieve your goals. Set specific, achievable goals that require effort to reach, and track the progress to ensure your effort is directed toward the most impactful tasks. Recognizing the value of hard work and perseverance, and celebrating these efforts, will reinforce the belief that abilities can be honed and expanded with time and dedication.

Continue to Learn

The desire to learn is a fundamental pillar of a growth mindset. It's about being endlessly curious, constantly seeking out new knowledge, and relentlessly striving to improve. Try to view each day as an opportunity to learn something new. Whether it's mastering a new skill at work, delving into a subject you've always been interested in, or even learning a fun new recipe, embrace the joy of learning.

Cultivate Persistence

Persistence is the lifeblood of a growth mindset. It's the willingness to keep going even when things get tough. When met with challenges, instead of retreating into the comfort of the known, individuals with a growth mindset repeatedly lean into the discomfort. It's habitual for them.

Persistence in a growth mindset is about understanding that worthwhile achievements demand time and effort. It's about appreciating the journey as much as the destination, valuing the process and not just the outcome. It encourages a healthy perspective on failure, viewing setbacks not as the end of the road, but as valuable feedback and an integral part of the growth process.

Seek Out Constructive Feedback

The ability to accept and act upon constructive criticism is crucial for adopting a growth mindset. It provides an outside perspective that can highlight blind spots and opportunities for growth. Feedback is your friend—it's a tool for growth, not a personal attack.

Learning to seek out and be receptive to constructive feedback is a crucial step in cultivating a growth mindset. Look for mentors, coaches, or colleagues who can provide you with insightful critiques. Use their feedback to refine your strategies, improve your skills, and push you toward success.

· · ·

Surround Yourself With Growth-Minded People

You're the sum of the company you keep. Surrounding yourself with people who also have a growth mindset can greatly impact your journey. Their positive attitudes, resilience in the face of challenges, and constant pursuit of growth can inspire and motivate you. Plus, they can provide invaluable support, advice, and encouragement as you navigate your own path to growth.

Celebrate Your Small Wins And The Success Of Others

Embracing a growth mindset involves taking inspiration from the success of others, rather than viewing it as a threat. Celebrate the achievements of your peers and consider what you can learn from their journey. By observing how they accomplished something, the strategies they employed, and how they can be applied or adapted to your situation, you'll be able to blossom alongside them. Using your surroundings for inspiration is an amazing and enriching experience.

Most importantly, celebrate each small win and success of your own! Don't sell yourself short just because you see others sharing large achievements. Having gratitude for your steady growth is how you will build the strength to keep going.

From Setbacks to Comebacks

Alright, let's get real here. Relationships are like a roller-coaster ride—full of ups, downs, twists, and turns. But sometimes, those twists and turns can lead to unexpected setbacks that leave us feeling lost and heartbroken. Whether it's communication issues, trust issues, or just the everyday struggles of maintaining a healthy relationship, we've all been there. So, let's get into some common relationship problems and explore how to navigate them like a pro.

Communication Breakdowns

One of the biggest culprits behind relationship problems? Poor communication. When we fail to communicate effectively with our partners, misunderstandings can arise, feelings can get hurt, and resentments can build. It's like playing a game of telephone where the message gets lost in translation.

So, how can you tackle this common issue? Start by fostering open and honest communication with your partner. Practice active listening, where you truly listen to what your partner is saying without interrupting or formulating your response. Validate their feelings, even if you don't necessarily agree with them. And don't be afraid to express your own needs and concerns in a calm and respectful manner.

For example, instead of sweeping problems under the rug, address them head-on. If you're feeling neglected because your partner spends too much time on their phone, have an open conversation about how you're feeling and brainstorm solutions together, like setting aside dedicated quality time without distractions.

Trust Issues

Another common relationship roadblock? Trust issues. Whether it's infidelity, past betrayals, or simply a lack of trust due to insecurities, trust issues can wreak havoc on even the strongest of relationships. When trust is broken, it can be incredibly challenging to rebuild.

So, how can you work through trust issues with your partner? It starts with open and transparent communication. Be honest about your concerns and fears, and encourage your partner to do the same. Establish boundaries and expectations together, and stick to them. And most importantly, be patient. Rebuilding trust takes time, effort, and consistency.

For instance, if you've been cheated on in the past and struggle with trust in your current relationship, consider seeking couples therapy. A qualified therapist can provide a safe space to explore your feelings, rebuild trust, and strengthen your bond as a couple.

Conflict Resolution

Let's face it—conflict is inevitable in any relationship. Whether it's a disagreement over finances, differing opinions on parenting, or simply clashing personalities, conflicts are bound to arise. But it's how we handle those conflicts that can make or break a relationship.

The key to effective conflict resolution? Communication, compromise, and compassion. Instead of resorting to yelling or name-calling, approach conflicts with a willingness to listen and understand your partner's perspective. Look for common ground and be open to finding solutions that work for both of you.

For example, if you and your partner constantly argue about household chores, sit down together and create a chore chart that divides responsibilities fairly. By working together to find a solution, you can prevent conflicts from escalating and strengthen your relationship in the process.

. . .

Intimacy Issues

Intimacy is a crucial component of any romantic relationship, but it's also one of the most vulnerable areas. Whether it's a lack of physical intimacy, emotional distance, or struggles with vulnerability, intimacy issues can create tension and strain in a relationship.

To address intimacy issues, start by having an open and honest conversation with your partner about your needs and desires. Be vulnerable and transparent about your feelings, and encourage your partner to do the same. Create opportunities for intimacy, whether it's through quality time together, meaningful conversations, or physical affection.

For instance, if you and your partner have been feeling disconnected lately, plan a romantic date night or a weekend getaway to reignite the spark in your relationship. By prioritizing intimacy and connection, you can strengthen your bond and overcome any obstacles standing in your way.

Financial Strain

Money matters can be a major source of stress and tension in relationships. Whether it's disagreements over spending habits, financial insecurity, or differing financial goals, financial strain can put a serious strain on even the strongest of partnerships.

To tackle financial issues head-on, start by having an open and honest conversation about your finances with your partner. Create a budget together, set financial goals, and establish clear expectations around money management. Be willing to compromise and make sacrifices for the greater good of your relationship.

For example, if you and your partner have different spending habits, consider setting up separate spending accounts for discretionary purchases while maintaining a joint account for shared expenses. This way, you can each maintain financial autonomy while still working toward your shared goals as a couple.

Thus, setbacks in relationships are inevitable, but they don't have to spell the end of your love story. By addressing common relationship problems head-on, fostering open communication, and working together as a team, you can navigate any obstacle that comes your way and emerge stronger and more resilient than ever. So, roll up your sleeves, put in the work, and get ready for your ultimate relationship comeback.

As we wrap up this journey of resilience and growth, we've witnessed how challenges can shape us into stronger, wiser versions of ourselves. Now, our narrative takes a turn toward the final chapter. Join us as we delve into the art of cultivating enduring habits, serving as a shield to safeguard your heart. These habits will not only guide you through healing but also fortify you with wisdom and resilience for the adventures that lie ahead. So, gear up for the final leg of our journey, where I'll equip you with the tools you need to embrace life's uncertainties with grace and strength.

7

M—MONUMENTALIZE YOUR HEALING

Let today be the day you give up who you've been for who you can become.

— HAL ELROD

This chapter isn't just about moving on from heartbreak; it's about evolving into a version of yourself that's stronger, wiser, and more resilient than ever before. We're diving into the realm of cultivating habits that will not only safeguard your heart but also ensure that you never find yourself in the depths of heartache again. So, grab a pen and paper, open your heart to the possibilities ahead, and let's pave the way for a future filled with love, joy, and monumental healing.

How Routine Can Help Us Conquer Heartbreak

You see, when your world feels like it's been turned upside down by the tumultuous waves of heartache, routine can be your anchor, keeping you steady amidst the storm.

Consistency Amid Chaos

In the aftermath of heartbreak, life can feel like a chaotic whirlwind of emotions. One day, you're swimming in a sea of sadness; the next, you're grappling with anger, and then there are moments when you're simply adrift in a fog of confusion. Amidst this emotional turbulence, establishing a daily routine provides much-needed consistency. It offers a sense of stability in an otherwise unpredictable world, grounding you and providing a comforting rhythm to your days.

A Sense of Purpose

When you're nursing a broken heart, it's easy to feel lost and adrift, unsure of where to turn or what to do next. That's where routine comes in handy. By mapping out your days with specific tasks and activities, you give yourself a sense of purpose. Each morning, when you wake up knowing exactly what lies ahead, it can infuse your days with a renewed sense of direction and meaning, helping you navigate through the darkest of times.

Mindful Moments of Self-Care

In the midst of heartbreak, it's crucial to prioritize self-care, but it's often easier said than done. That's where routine comes to the rescue once again. By incorporating regular self-care practices into your daily schedule, such as meditation, exercise, or simply indulging in your favorite hobby, you create dedicated moments of solace and rejuvenation amidst the chaos. These mindful moments not only soothe your soul but also remind you of the importance of prioritizing your own well-being, even in the midst of heartache.

Building Confidence and Resilience

As you navigate the rocky terrain of heartbreak, every small victory counts. Establishing a routine and sticking to it, day in and day out, is a testament to your strength and resilience. Each time you tick off a task on your daily to-do list, you're affirming your ability to persevere in the face of adversity. Over time, this builds confidence in your resilience, reminding you that no matter how tough things may seem, you have the inner strength to weather the storm and emerge stronger on the other side.

Examples of Routine in Action

Let's say you've decided to incorporate a morning walk into your daily routine. Every morning, rain or shine, you lace up your sneakers and head out for a brisk stroll around the neighborhood. As you breathe in the fresh air and feel the sun on your face, you're not just exercising your body; you're also nourishing your soul. This simple routine becomes a source of solace and rejuvenation, grounding you and setting a positive tone for the rest of the day.

Or perhaps you've allocated some time each evening for journaling. As you sit down with pen and paper in hand, you pour out your thoughts and emotions onto the page, allowing yourself to process and make sense of the whirl-wind of feelings swirling inside you. Through this consistent practice of self-reflection, you gain clarity and insight, empowering you to navigate the complexities of heartbreak with grace and resilience.

Thus, don't underestimate the transformative power of routine in healing from heartbreak. By providing stability, purpose, and moments of self-care, routine can be your steadfast companion on the journey toward healing and wholeness.

Heart-Friendly Habits to Beat Heartache

Let's dive into one of the toughest yet most crucial aspects of healing from heartbreak: emotionally detaching from someone you love but shouldn't or can't be with. It's like navigating through a maze of emotions, but trust me, finding your way out is possible, and it starts with understanding when and how to emotionally detach.

Knowing When to Let Go

Emotionally detaching from someone you love can feel like tearing off a piece of your own heart. It's a painful process that often requires immense courage and self-awareness. But how do you know when it's time to let go? Well, if the relationship is causing you more pain than joy, if you find yourself constantly sacrificing your own well-being for the sake of someone else, or if you've realized that the relationship is simply not healthy or sustainable, then it may be time to consider emotional detachment.

How to Emotionally Detach

Detaching emotionally doesn't mean shutting off your feelings like a faucet. It's a gradual process of creating space between yourself and the person you need to let go of. Start by setting boundaries and limiting contact with them, whether it's in person, over the phone, or on social media. Focus on redirecting your energy toward activities and relationships that nourish your soul and bring you joy. And most importantly, practice self-compassion and patience with yourself as you navigate through the waves of grief and longing.

Let's say you've realized that staying in touch with your ex is only prolonging your heartache and hindering your healing process. It's time to take a step back and emotionally detach. You might start by muting their social media posts or limiting the time you spend reminiscing about the past. Instead, focus on nurturing your own well-being by spending time with supportive friends, engaging in activities you love, and practicing self-care. It won't be easy, and there may be moments when you feel tempted to reach out to them, but remember that emotional detachment is a journey, and every small step forward is a victory in itself.

Make Self-Care a Priority

Now that we've discussed the importance of emotionally detaching and creating space for healing, let's shift our focus to another essential aspect of overcoming heartache: self-care. In the midst of heartbreak, it's easy to neglect your own well-being, but prioritizing self-care is key to nurturing your mental and emotional health.

Self-care is more than just bubble baths and face masks (although those can be great, too!). At its core, self-care is about intentionally taking care of your physical, emotional, and mental needs to maintain overall well-being. It's about treating yourself with the same kindness and compassion you would offer to a friend in need.

The benefits of self-care extend far beyond momentary relaxation. It can reduce stress, improve mood, boost self-esteem, and enhance resilience—all of which are crucial for healing from heartbreak.

Starting a self-care routine doesn't have to be complicated or time-consuming. Begin by identifying activities that bring you joy and make you feel grounded. Whether it's going for a walk in nature, practicing mindfulness meditation, or indulging in your favorite hobby, carve out time in your schedule for self-care and treat it as non-negotiable.

When it comes to self-care for mental wellbeing, the possibilities are endless. You might try journaling to express your thoughts and feelings, practicing deep breathing exercises to calm your mind, or engaging in creative activities like painting or writing poetry. Surrounding yourself with uplifting music, spending time with loved ones who make you laugh, or even seeking professional support through therapy are also valuable forms of self-care.

Imagine you've had a particularly challenging day filled with waves of sadness and longing for your past relationship. Instead of spiraling into despair, you decide to practice self-care. You take a break from your responsibilities and spend the evening cuddled up with a good book, sipping your favorite herbal tea, and allowing yourself to unwind. In that moment, you're showing yourself the kindness and compassion you deserve, nurturing your mental well-being one small act at a time.

Think Positive Thoughts

In the midst of heartache, it can be challenging to maintain a positive outlook, but fostering a mindset of positivity can be a powerful tool for healing. Let's explore what positive thinking entails and how it can benefit you on your journey toward healing.

Positive thinking involves deliberately focusing on the bright side of situations and maintaining an optimistic attitude, even in the face of adversity. It's about reframing negative thoughts and finding silver linings, no matter how small they may seem.

The benefits of positive thinking extend beyond just feeling happier. It can reduce stress, improve resilience, boost self-esteem, and enhance overall well-being. By cultivating a positive mindset, you're better equipped to navigate life's challenges and bounce back from setbacks with greater ease.

Practicing positive thinking is a skill that can be developed over time with conscious effort and mindfulness. Start by paying attention to your thoughts and actively challenging negative or pessimistic beliefs. Whenever you catch yourself dwelling on what went wrong or catastrophizing about the future, pause and reframe the situation in a more positive light.

Imagine you're feeling overwhelmed by loneliness and longing for your ex-partner. Instead of wallowing in despair, you consciously choose to think positively. You remind yourself of the friendships and support systems you have in your life, focusing on the love and connection that surrounds you. You tell yourself that this period of heartbreak is temporary and that brighter days are ahead. By shifting your perspective and embracing positivity, you're able to find solace and hope in the midst of pain.

Find an Outlet for Negative Emotions

In the wake of heartbreak, it's natural to experience a whirlwind of negative emotions—from sadness and anger to frustration and despair. Finding a healthy outlet to channel and release these emotions is crucial for your mental and emotional well-being. Let's explore the difference between unhealthy and healthy outlets and discover how you can effectively release negative emotions.

Unhealthy outlets for negative emotions often involve

behaviors that provide temporary relief but ultimately exacerbate your pain or harm yourself and others. Examples include excessive drinking, substance abuse, reckless behavior, or lashing out at loved ones. These outlets may offer short-term distraction or numbness, but they only prolong the healing process and create additional problems.

On the other hand, healthy outlets for negative emotions allow you to acknowledge and express your feelings constructively, leading to genuine healing and growth. Examples include journaling, exercising, engaging in creative activities like painting or music, practicing mindfulness or meditation, talking to a trusted friend or therapist, or volunteering for a cause you care about. These outlets provide a safe space for processing emotions and offer opportunities for catharsis and self-discovery.

Finding the right outlet for your negative emotions may require some trial and error, but it's worth the effort to discover what works best for you. Start by exploring different activities or practices that resonate with you and allow you to express yourself authentically. Pay attention to how each outlet makes you feel and whether it helps alleviate your emotional burden.

Once you've identified a healthy outlet, make it a regular part of your routine. Set aside dedicated time each day or week to engage in your chosen activity or practice. Consistency is key to reaping the full benefits of emotional release and finding relief from heartache.

Revenge Won't Make You Feel Better
When you're nursing a broken heart, it's normal to feel a surge of anger and the urge to seek revenge on your ex-partner. However, indulging in revenge fantasies or actions

rarely brings the satisfaction you crave and often leaves you feeling emptier than before.

Here are some tips on how you can channel your vindictive energy to more positive things:

- **Focus on self-improvement:** Instead of dwelling on ways to get back at your ex, redirect your energy toward personal growth and development. Use this opportunity to invest in yourself—take up a new hobby, enroll in a course, or focus on advancing your career. By prioritizing your own well-being and success, you shift the focus away from seeking revenge and toward building a brighter future for yourself.

- **Practice forgiveness:** While it may seem counterintuitive, forgiveness is a powerful antidote to vindictiveness. Holding onto resentment only prolongs your pain and keeps you tethered to the past. Choose to forgive your ex-partner, not because they deserve it, but because you deserve peace. By letting go of grudges and releasing negative energy, you free yourself to move forward with a lighter heart.

- **Channel emotions creatively:** Transform your feelings of anger and betrayal into creative expression. Write poetry or songs, paint or draw, dance, or engage in any form of artistic expression that allows you to release pent-up emotions in a constructive way. Channeling your vindictive energy into creativity not only provides catharsis but also fosters a sense of empowerment and resilience.

- **Focus on positivity and gratitude:** Shift your perspective from dwelling on the hurtful actions of your ex-partner to focusing on the positive aspects of your life. Practice gratitude daily by reflecting on the things you're thankful for, whether it's supportive friends and family, moments of joy, or personal achievements. Cultivating a positive mindset helps counteract feelings of vindictiveness and fosters a sense of inner peace and contentment.

While revenge may seem tempting in the aftermath of heartbreak, it ultimately perpetuates negativity and prolongs your suffering.

Practice Gratitude

Gratitude is like a beacon of light in the darkness of despair—a powerful antidote to the pain of heartbreak. But what exactly is gratitude, and why is it so crucial in the healing process?

Gratitude is more than just saying "thank you"; it's a deep sense of appreciation for the blessings in your life, both big and small. It's about recognizing the goodness that surrounds you, even in the midst of difficult times. When you practice gratitude, you cultivate a mindset of abundance and positivity, shifting your focus from what's lacking to what you have.

In the aftermath of heartbreak, it's easy to become consumed by negative emotions and dwell on the pain of loss. However, practicing gratitude helps counteract these feelings by fostering a sense of perspective and resilience. By acknowledging the things you're grateful for, you invite more positivity into your life and strengthen your emotional well-being. Gratitude also has numerous physical and psychological benefits, from reducing stress and anxiety to improving sleep and overall happiness.

Let's take a look at some ways to practice gratitude:

- Start each day by writing down three things you're grateful for. They can be as simple as a warm cup of coffee in the morning, a supportive friend, or a beautiful sunset. Reflecting on these blessings helps shift your mindset toward gratitude and sets a positive tone for the day ahead.
- Take the time to express gratitude to those around you who have supported you during your healing journey. Send a heartfelt thank-you note, give someone a sincere compliment, or simply tell them how much you appreciate their presence in your life. Genuine expressions of gratitude not only strengthen your relationships but also uplift your spirits.
- Incorporate mindfulness practices into your daily routine, such as mindful breathing or body scans. Pay attention to the present moment and notice the beauty and abundance that surrounds you. Cultivating mindfulness allows you to fully experience and appreciate life's blessings, no matter how small.
- Before going to bed, take a moment to reflect on the events of the day and identify moments of gratitude. Recall the positive experiences, acts of kindness, or moments of joy that you encountered. Focusing on these blessings before

sleep helps quiet the mind and promotes a
restful night's sleep.

Unhealthy Relationship Habits to Break Right Now

Breaking free from the cycle of heartbreak often requires
identifying and dismantling unhealthy relationship habits
that may have contributed to your pain. Let's shine a light
on these habits and explore why it's essential to bid them
farewell.

Self-Sacrifice Over Self-Care

One of the most detrimental habits in relationships is
prioritizing the needs of others at the expense of your own
well-being. Constantly sacrificing your own happiness and
neglecting self-care can lead to feelings of resentment,
exhaustion, and ultimately, heartbreak. Remember, you
can't pour from an empty cup. It's crucial to prioritize your
own self-care and set healthy boundaries to ensure your
needs are met.

Ignoring Red Flags

Ignoring or rationalizing red flags in a relationship is a
recipe for heartbreak. Whether it's overlooking disre-
spectful behavior, minimizing your partner's flaws, or
excusing recurring conflicts, turning a blind eye to warning
signs only prolongs inevitable pain. Instead, trust your intuition and take heed of any behavior that undermines your
emotional well-being. Addressing red flags early on can save
you from future heartache.

People-Pleasing

Constantly seeking validation and approval from your
partner by bending over backward to meet their expectations is a harmful habit that erodes your sense of self-worth.
Suppressing your true thoughts, feelings, and desires to
avoid conflict or maintain harmony in the relationship leads

to emotional suppression and resentment. Authenticity is the cornerstone of healthy relationships, so embrace your true self and communicate openly with your partner.

Lack of Communication

Communication is the lifeblood of any successful relationship, yet many fall into the trap of avoiding difficult conversations or sweeping issues under the rug. Bottling up emotions, avoiding confrontation, or resorting to passive-aggressive behavior only breeds resentment and misunderstanding. Instead, cultivate open, honest communication with your partner, even when it feels uncomfortable. Addressing concerns and expressing your needs openly fosters trust, intimacy, and mutual understanding.

Dependency

Relying excessively on your partner for validation, happiness, and fulfillment sets the stage for codependency and emotional instability. While it's natural to seek support from your partner, placing your entire sense of self-worth and happiness in their hands is unsustainable and unhealthy. Cultivate independence, pursue your passions, and nurture your own identity outside of the relationship. Remember, you are whole and complete on your own.

Identifying and breaking free from these unhealthy relationship habits is an empowering step toward healing from heartbreak and fostering healthier connections in the future.

Hacks to Help You Stick to Your Habits

Forming new habits can be challenging, especially when navigating the aftermath of heartbreak. However, with the right strategies and mindset, you can set yourself up for success. Let's explore some practical hacks to help you stick to your habits and create lasting positive change in your life.

Start Small

When embarking on a habit-forming journey, it's tempting to dive in headfirst and set lofty goals. However, starting small is often more effective in the long run. Break down your larger objectives into smaller, manageable tasks that you can incorporate into your daily routine. For example, if your goal is to prioritize self-care, start by dedicating just 10 minutes each day to a relaxing activity like meditation or journaling.

Create a Routine

Consistency is key when forming new habits. Establishing a daily routine can help reinforce your desired behaviors and make them feel more automatic over time. Designate specific times each day for practicing your habits, whether it's exercising in the morning, practicing gratitude before bed, or setting aside time for self-reflection during lunch breaks. Consistently sticking to your routine will gradually solidify your habits and make them second nature.

Use Visual Reminders

Visual cues can serve as powerful reminders to engage in your desired habits. Place visual reminders, such as sticky notes, motivational quotes, or symbols related to your habits, in prominent places where you'll see them throughout the day. For instance, if you're striving to cultivate a positive mindset, place uplifting affirmations on your bathroom mirror or set a screensaver with motivational quotes on your phone.

Track Your Progress

Tracking your progress allows you to monitor your success and stay motivated along the way. Keep a habit tracker journal or use mobile apps to record your daily activities and mark off each successful completion. Celebrate your wins, no matter how small, and use your progress as fuel to keep moving forward. Seeing tangible evidence of your growth can boost your confidence and reinforce your commitment to your habits.

Practice Accountability

Enlist the support of friends, family, or accountability partners to help you stay accountable to your goals. Share your intentions with someone you trust and ask them to check in on your progress regularly. Having someone to share your successes and setbacks with can provide encouragement, motivation, and an added layer of accountability to keep you on track.

Incorporate these hacks into your daily life, and watch as your habits become ingrained behaviors that contribute to your healing journey and overall well-being. Remember, consistency and persistence are key, so be patient with yourself and celebrate your progress along the way.

AFTERWORD

I am so proud of you, dear reader, that you have reached the conclusion of this transformative journey toward healing from heartbreak. As you reflect on the ups and downs, the triumphs and setbacks, I want you to take a moment to acknowledge the strength and resilience that resides within you. You've navigated through the stormy seas of heartache, facing challenges head-on and emerging stronger on the other side. Your journey may have been arduous, but it has led you to this pivotal moment of growth and self-discovery.

Throughout this book, we've explored the depths of pain and sorrow that accompany heartbreak, but we've also delved into the boundless potential for healing and renewal that lies within each of us. You've set off on a journey of self-exploration, learning to embrace your emotions, reclaim your identity, and cultivate self-love in the face of adversity. Along the way, you've discovered the power of vulnerability, the importance of forgiveness, and the beauty of resilience.

But your healing journey doesn't end here—it's an ongoing process, a continual evolution toward self-empowerment and inner peace. As you navigate the complexities of life, you'll encounter new challenges, triumphs, and moments of profound growth. Embrace each experience as an opportunity to deepen your understanding of yourself and the world around you. Remember, healing is not linear; it's a journey marked by twists and turns, peaks and valleys. Allow yourself the grace to stumble, to falter, and to learn from every setback. With each step forward, you're not just healing from past wounds; you're forging a stronger, more resilient version of yourself.

As we part ways, I want to leave you with a few guiding principles to carry with you on your journey:

- **Embrace imperfection:** Healing is not a linear process, and it's okay to stumble along the way. Embrace your imperfections, for they are what make you beautifully human. Allow yourself the grace to make mistakes, learn from them, and grow stronger as a result.

- **Practice self-compassion:** Be gentle with yourself as you navigate the twists and turns of your healing journey. Treat yourself with the same kindness and understanding that you would offer to a dear friend facing similar challenges. Remember that you are deserving of love, acceptance, and compassion, especially during times of struggle.

- **Cultivate gratitude:** In moments of darkness, it can be easy to lose sight of the blessings that surround us. Take time each day to cultivate gratitude for the simple joys and blessings in your life. Whether it's a beautiful sunrise, a heartfelt conversation, or a warm cup of tea, find moments of gratitude to anchor you amidst the storm.

- **Embrace your authentic self:** You are a unique and multifaceted individual worthy of love and belonging just as you are. Embrace your authenticity, quirks and all, and celebrate the essence of who you are. Remember that true healing begins when we embrace our authentic selves and live in alignment with our values and desires.
- **Keep moving forward:** Healing is a journey, not a destination, and it's important to keep moving forward, even when the path ahead seems uncertain. Trust in your resilience, your inner strength, and your ability to overcome whatever obstacles may come your way. With each step you take, you are inching closer toward a brighter, more fulfilling future.

As we bid farewell to this chapter of your healing journey, know that the lessons you've learned and the growth you've experienced will serve as guiding lights in the days, weeks, and months to come. Prepare to start the next chapter of your life with newfound courage, wisdom, and resilience, knowing that you have the power to create a future filled with love, joy, and endless possibilities.

In closing, dear reader, I want to express my deepest gratitude for allowing me to be a part of your healing journey. If this book has touched your heart, inspired you to embrace your healing journey, or helped you rediscover the love and strength within you, I invite you to share your thoughts with others. Your review could be the guiding light that leads someone else to the path of renewed happiness and inner peace.

May your heart be light, your spirit be strong, and your journey be filled with boundless hope and endless healing. You've got this, dear reader. Embrace your healing journey with open arms, and watch as the beauty of transformation unfolds before your eyes.

BIBLIOGRAPHY

5 reasons why it's hard to forgive people. (n.d.). Psych2Go. https://psych2go.net/5-reasons-hard-forgive-people/

A quote by Ann Landers. (n.d.). Www.goodreads.com. Retrieved March 23, 2024, from https://www.goodreads.com/quotes/17642-some-people-believe-holding-on-and-hanging-in-there-are

A quote by Charles Bukowski. (n.d.). Www.goodreads.com. https://www.goodreads.com/quotes/6946540-if-you-have-the-ability-to-love-love-yourself-first

A quote by Ralph Waldo Emerson. (n.d.). Www.goodreads.com. Retrieved March 28, 2024, from https://www.goodreads.com/quotes/13654-we-acquire-the-strength-we-have-overcome

Cherry, K. (2023, February 20). *How to forgive yourself.* Verywell Mind. https://www.verywellmind.com/how-to-forgive-yourself-4583819

Coelho, P. (n.d.). *A quote from The Zahir.* Www.goodreads.com. Retrieved March 22, 2024, from https://www.goodreads.com/quotes/57799-when-someone-leaves-it-s-because-someone-else-is-about-to

Hal Elrod quote. (n.d.). A-Z Quotes. Retrieved March 28, 2024, from https://www.azquotes.com/quote/1033548

Kromberg, J. (2013). *The 5 stages of grieving the end of a relationship.* Psychology Today. https://www.psychologytoday.com/us/blog/inside-out/201309/the-5-stages-grieving-the-end-relationship

Mathews, A. (2016, March 12). *What does it mean to let go?* Www.psychology-today.com. https://www.psychologytoday.com/intl/blog/traversing-the-inner-terrain/201603/what-does-it-mean-let-go

Matveyeva, A. (2021, July 28). *101 productivity quotes to keep you inspired at work.* Chanty. https://www.chanty.com/blog/productivity-quotes/

Ribeiro, M. (2019, April 9). *How to be mentally strong: 14 ways to build mental toughness.* PositivePsychology.com. https://positivepsychology.com/mentally-strong

Robert Breault quote: "In the end you don't so much find yourself as you find someone who knows who you are." (n.d.). Quotefancy.com. https://quotefancy.com/quote/1579397/Robert-Breault-In-the-end-you-don-t-so-much-find-yourself-as-you-find-someone-who-knows

Rodriguez, C. (2021, April 29). *Depression and fatigue: Why it happens and how to cope.* Psych Central. https://psychcentral.com/depression/depression-and-fatigue

The importance of forgiving yourself and others. (n.d.). Www.counselling-Directory.org.uk. https://www.counselling-directory.org.uk/memberarticles/the-importance-of-forgiving-yourself-others

The Storyteller Quotes by Jodi Picoult. (n.d.). Www.goodreads.com. Retrieved March 23, 2024, from https://www.goodreads.com/work/quotes/21449403-the-storyteller#:~:text=Forgiving%20isn

Printed in Dunstable, United Kingdom

66258849R00080